A Good News Spirituality

A Good News Spirituality

Finding Holiness in Parish Life

JOHN BURKE, O.P.

PAULIST PRESS
New York/Mahwah, N.J.

Cover design by Lundgren Graphics

Library of Congress Cataloging-in-Publication Data

Burke, John, 1928-
    A good news spirituality : finding holiness in parish life / John Burke.
        p.   cm.
    Includes bibliographical references.
    ISBN 0-8091-3963-4 (alk. paper)
        1. Christian ethics—Catholic authors. 2. Holiness—Catholic Church.
    3. Catholic preaching. I. Title
BJ1249.B86 2000
241'.042—dc21

                                                                    00-028544

Published by Paulist Press
997 Macarthur Boulevard
Mahwah, New Jersey 07430

www.paulistpress.com

Printed and bound in the
United States of America

Contents

Acknowledgments

I wish to acknowledge my fellow scholars, colleagues and friends who have helped me so much in the writing of this book. It has turned out to be far more demanding than I had originally envisioned, and without their assistance I could not have accomplished it. Writing on moral matters today is a demanding task, and writing on preaching is a responsible one. As a result, I consulted with many people at various stages of the book's evolution, and each one contributed importantly to the final product. At the same time, of course, only I can be held responsible for the book's contents, which are in full agreement with the teaching of the Roman Catholic Church.

In particular, I would like to thank my Dominican confreres, Benedict M. Ashley, Robert Barry, Basil Cole and Aaron Laushway, for their careful reading of the manuscript and their excellent observations regarding it. Fr. John Harvey, OSFS, was especially helpful to me. Jack Wright and Mary Sheehy made excellent comments, which kept me on the right track with regard to the readership I hope to enrich.

Subsequently, the book was shaped by comments by Professor William C. Cenkner of The Catholic University of America, Claire Breault, former editor of *The GoodNews Letter* of the National Institute for the Word of God, and Mike Ryman, an Advisor to the Institute.

My thanks also to Tara Brazee Hoover, research librarian of the Dominican House of Studies Library, and Patrick Pettit, Associate Director and Head of Public Services of the Law Library of The Catholic University of America.

Abbreviations

CA	=	*Centesimus Annus*, John Paul II
CCC	=	*Catechism of the Catholic Church*
CSL	=	*Constitution on the Sacred Liturgy*, Vatican II
EN	=	*Evangelii Nuntiandi*, Paul VI
ST	=	*Summa Theologiae*, Thomas Aquinas

Introduction

$\mathcal{T}$he purpose of this book is to help all who share in any way the ministry of the word in a Catholic parish to communicate the moral teaching of the gospel of Jesus Christ in a way that enables the people who listen to hear it as "the good news of salvation." While people are searching for moral guidance in their daily affairs, they are not hungering simply for rules of morality. They hunger, deeply, for a richer life—a life of joy and peace and serenity—of which morality is a constitutive element.

The Sunday Homily Cannot Do It All

The Sunday homily is certainly the preeminent form of preaching in the Roman Catholic tradition; nevertheless, it is not the only form of preaching.[1] In addition to the ordained— bishops, priests and deacons—lay persons can be and are being authorized to preach, even in churches.[2] In parish after parish, communicating the gospel of Jesus Christ is becoming more and more a team ministry, made up not only of ordained clergy, but also of lay persons working with them. As catechists and evangelists,[3] lay Catholics are witnessing in a powerful way to the movement of the Holy Spirit in the church. They serve as directors of religious education programs, as catechists for both children and adults, and as sponsors in the

1

RCIA, and in those parishes that have outreach programs to non-Catholics they are serving in the front line as evangelists. All this parish team ministry is done in full cooperation with parents,[4] the first teachers of their children. Indeed, parents in a most true sense are probably not only the first but also the most important preachers their children ever hear.[5] When all of these individuals in a parish work together to make Jesus known, believed and trusted, the believer is made one with the Father (Jn 14:23).

As in all times past, the Catholic Church speaks out forcefully on moral matters, although large numbers do not seem to hear the church's teaching as good news. However, others, both Catholics and non-Catholics, are listening, and they look to the church for guidance. To win a welcome hearing from free men and women, the parish team needs to situate the church's teaching on human behavior in the perspective of divine love—namely, all human beings are called to become holy and thereby image God himself. This kind of communication will enable contemporary listeners to have a deeper respect for the church's rich teaching on morality with all its positive ramifications for human love and growth in gospel joy.

Veritatis Splendor Restores Confidence in Church Teaching

Pope John Paul II helped Catholic parishes proclaim Catholic moral teaching as the good news of salvation when on August 6, 1993 he issued an encyclical letter, the *Splendor of Truth*,[6] "to all the bishops of the Catholic Church regarding certain fundamental questions of the church's moral teaching. According to the pope, "Today, it seems necessary to reflect on the whole of the church's moral teaching, with the precise goal of recalling certain fundamental truths of Catholic doctrine, which in the present circumstances risk being distorted or denied" (n. 4). Then he goes on to state the specific purpose of the encyclical very clearly: "The specific purpose of the present encyclical is this: to set forth, with regard to the problems being discussed, the principles of a moral teaching based upon sacred scripture and the living apostolic tradition, and at the same time to shed light on the presuppositions and consequences of the dissent which that teaching has encountered" (n. 5).

Morality Needs To Be Communicated from the Perspective of Divine Love

Many do not appreciate the church's moral teaching because frequently parish leaders have not presented it in an attractive and therefore persuasive manner. The parish team cannot pass on the church's exalted moral tradition that has so much insight into the human heart by reducing it to negatives. This is especially true today when our society has developed an intense sensitivity to human dignity that requires each of us to respect the personal decisions and privacy of others.

No one has ever been able to command or legislate morality. Popes, kings and parents can command and legislate external compliance, but the inner reaches of the human heart can only be won over by goodness and truth. Parents may be able to coerce behavioral conformity in their children for a time, but once the child has reached maturity, if the parents' teachings have not found a receptive home in the child's heart, the adult child will abandon those teachings once he or she is free of the parents' external constraints.

To win a welcome hearing from free men and women, the parish team needs to situate the church's teaching on human behavior in the perspective of divine love: namely, all human beings are called to become holy and thereby image God. This kind of communication will enable contemporary listeners to have a deeper respect for the church's rich teachings on morality with all its positive ramifications for human love and growth in gospel joy.

While not neglecting more traditional academic and systematic approaches to Christian ethics and morality, the team needs to emphasize in their ordinary communication of the gospel the joy of moral living. If they do, the parish is more apt to be convinced of the validity of the church's teachings and thus "have life and have it more abundantly" (Jn 10:10).

The Parish Ministry: Make People Want To Be Holy

Put in the simplest terms, the heart of the thesis of this book is that in order to communicate Christian morality today, those responsible for doing so—priests, deacons, catechists, evangelists, and parents—need to hold up for each listener, whether child, teenager, or adult, an attainable vision of holiness in such a way that each will hunger to be holy. We are made in the image of God, and God is holy. Therefore, it follows that the goal of each person's life is to order every action toward making himself or herself holy.[7] Only when human beings are holy in the image of God will they be personally happy and at peace with themselves and with others.

From this it follows that we can appreciate and value the demands of the divine Law only when we are striving to reflect the holiness of God, for conformity to the law makes us holy. The precepts of the divine Law are revealed to us through our own innate sense of right and wrong (conscience), the teaching of scripture and the tradition of the church.

It Is Difficult To Establish Holiness as a Norm Today

Our American society operates on three principles which form a kind of religious basis for its activities and values. They form a "religious" basis because they are fundamental assumptions that are not really questioned but are very pervasive in their influence.

The first principle is that all truth is relative. No single authority can say that what is true for him or her is true for everyone. Rather, it is up to each person to decide what is true for him or her.

The second principle is that since all truth is relative, there is no universal moral law that is binding on all. Rather, each person has to make a choice about what is right or wrong.

Finally, these two principles assume that this earthly world is the only world, and, therefore, that success in this world is the only thing that truly matters.[8]

It is easy to see that as a result of the general acceptance, perhaps even subconsciously, of these operative principles, the value of holiness as a moral norm is underestimated. Secular culture today has clouded our understanding of the evil of sin and has gone so far as to even deny the existence of sin.[9] The effect of sin can been seen in the substitution of a weak, sentimental understanding of love in the popular mind that, in fact, destroys the scriptural notion of love which is founded on the absolute holiness of God.[10]

Therefore, to be effective, the parish needs to establish in the hearts and minds of the faithful, of whatever age, education or social condition, the absolute holiness of God. The team needs to make vivid what holiness is by vividly depicting God's holiness as revealed in the Bible.

God's Holiness Is Revealed in Power and Love

In the Old Testament, God's holiness is revealed in striking images of power as well as by stories of his love of his chosen people. In the New Testament, the biblical idea of holiness is expressed most perfectly in the life, death and resurrection of Jesus Christ, especially in his sacrificial death on the cross. Jesus' death reveals both God's power and love as well as the evil of sin, which was the cause of his crucifixion.

At the Last Supper Jesus prepares his disciples for his death, saying to them:

> The world must know that I love the Father and that I do just as the Father has commanded me (Jn 14:31).

And then he prays to his Father, the Most Holy One, that he will give his disciples the holy love that is in God himself. In fact, the love of God in Jesus' disciples will be the great sign that Jesus is from God and that God's love is in all who believe (Jn 17:21-26).

In the light of this revelation of God's holiness, members of the parish formation team need to portray with equal vividness the antithesis of holiness, which is sin. Scripture and the teaching of the church reveal lucidly both what sin is and deleterious effects it has on human life.[11]

After the parish leaders have established the validity of the fundamental norm of holiness, then they need to reveal the sources of holiness, that is, the means by which Christians today can identify and overcome sin so that they are free to love as God loves and, thereby, become holy as God is holy.

This is accomplished through the communicating of the divine law, the whole purpose of which is to move people to holiness through faith in Christ Jesus. In fact, the divine plan of salvation through faith in Jesus Christ cannot really be valued unless the believer has an overwhelming sense of his or her own sinfulness, and, therefore, the need to be rescued from it. This is what salvation is: deliverance from the power of sin through the sacrificial death of Jesus Christ. Without a sense of need for forgiveness, one cannot really be saved. Without a sense of personal sinfulness, the blood of Christ has no real significance; for what we are saved from is sin.[12]

Here, in the making graphic of both holiness and sinfulness, is both the challenge and the opportunity that face Catholic parishes today.

Scripture and Notes Abound

In order not to interrupt the smooth flow of the text, but at the same time to provide adequate support for many of the statements affirmed, I have made abundant use of notes. I have also quoted scripture extensively, because scripture is the source not only of doctrine but of prayer. I hope that the texts quoted will help readers to connect the message of the book with prayer as they meditate on the meaning of the passages cited.

And so we begin our undertaking in faith with a prayer:

May the Holy Spirit of wisdom give the parish formation team knowledge and experience of the saving power of Jesus Christ and lead each of them ever more deeply into the mystery of the divine holiness of the Father. Amen.

1

The Perspective of the American
Catholic Listener

*I*n order to communicate the saving message of Jesus Christ, it is vital that the parish team take into account the various influences which shape how American Catholics hear the teaching of the church. The diversity of these influences results in a certain tension in individual Catholics as they seek to integrate their experience of the Catholic faith into their daily lives.

There are at least three factors that influence how American Catholics experience religion and arrive at a personal spirituality. The first is the contemporary American culture. The second is made up of all the practical aspects of daily living, especially the economic and political realities. Finally, there is the teaching of the church that is mediated primarily through catechetical formation and liturgical preaching and secondarily through various forms of printed and electronic media.

American Culture Shapes the Way Our Listeners Hear Our Message

One of the great heritages of American political life is the separation of church and state. As a result, religion is perceived by all Americans, including Catholics, as basically a private matter of individual judgment. Robert Bellah, for example, found that the interviews he and his associates conducted for their research project, *Habits of the Heart,* coincided with a Gallup poll of 1978 in which "80% of Americans agreed that an individual should arrive at his or her own religious beliefs independent of any churches or synagogues."[1]

Since religion is a matter of private preference, tolerance for the religious values of others has played a key role in American political and social life. It has also resulted in an extensive religious pluralism. American culture regards churches as voluntary organizations made up of members who agree on certain values and beliefs, and as long as the tenets and practices of any particular church are not in conflict with the values held by society as a whole, or harmful to its well-being, that church is given complete freedom. As a result, many churches can hold rather extreme doctrines and still remain free to engage in their religious activities. Even so bizarre a cult as that run by Jim Jones, whose followers committed suicide at his command in 1978, was able to preach his doctrine for years under the protection of the law.

On the other hand, if the doctrines are not in accord with generally held understandings and values, and are perceived to be in conflict with the general good, they may well meet legal opposition. So, for example, Protestant fundamentalists have been strongly rebuffed in court cases with regard to the teaching of creationism in the public schools.

In another action, the American Civil Liberties Union is challenging in court the tax-exempt status of the American Catholic bishops because of their political activities against abortion. What the eventual outcome of that suit will be is unclear at this time.

The point is that for Americans in general, the individual is ultimately the "source of all religious meaning." This is true even though the individual may be a member of a church group by reason of a voluntary association with it.[2] "Most

Americans see religion as something individual, prior to any organizational involvement."[3]

Because religion based on individual preference can only exist by mutual toleration, religion in America tends to stress the importance of respecting the rights of others to hold and publicize their views, as long as those views do not intrude on the rights of others. (This has tremendous ramifications for American Catholics' tolerance of abortion.)

Since fanaticism of all kinds, including and especially religious fanaticism, is decried by American society, American religion stresses benevolence toward all, yet without demanding serious efforts toward meeting their needs. With this understanding of religion, love is reduced to sentiment which is satisfied with "not hurting others."

Because much of American religion is so self-centered and because popular expressions of religious sentiment do not demand heroic service to others, religion gets most of its strength from the fact that it enables individuals to feel good about themselves so that they can cope with the pressures that come from a highly competitive society.

Bellah quotes one of his interviewees who sums up some forms of contemporary religious belief:

> Just try to love yourself and be gentle with yourself. You know, I guess, take care of each other. I think He would want us to take care of each other.[4]

Catholics have both benefited from religious tolerance and become leading practitioners of it. For example, they are more tolerant of racial and ethnic differences and sexual practices. Gallup reports:

> [Catholics] tend to regard sexual activities as matters of privacy which do not necessarily have any bearing on the political or social order; Catholics do not look to the law to enforce sexual morality.[5]

In fact, there is evidence that they become uneasy when church authorities try to influence their political activities to bring about a legislation of morality. Gallup reports that Catholics were not enthusiastic about the bishops' 1983 pastoral letter, "The Challenge of Peace: God's Promise and Our Response," or the consultation process which preceded its final issuance.

> Catholics firmly reject any church action that smacks of partisan politics or any form of political manipulation. And if that is the case, it is clear that the bishops [in the case of the peace pastoral] have not convinced their people that they are not getting involved in street level politics.[6]

This data concerning reaction to the peace pastoral is interesting, because while Catholics are popularly conceived as anti-communist, which they are, and might be expected to be hawkish, in fact they are not. "They have been doves for a generation and show no signs of reversing that thrust."[7]

At the same time, Catholics are in general agreement with their bishops regarding economics, favoring government regulation of the economy, sensitivity toward the poor, and redistribution of wealth through tax legislation. Briefly put, even though Catholics have entered into the middle class, their immigrant beginnings and their origins in poverty have kept them on the liberal side of economic issues.[8]

Nevertheless, when the bishops of the United States were holding extensive consultations in the development of their pastoral on the economy, "Catholic Social Teaching and the U.S. Economy," and even after its subsequent promulgation, many prominent Catholics, including a former U.S. Secretary of the Treasury, William Simon, vigorously dissented from the bishops' position and freely used the media to make known their opposition.[9]

In another case, while the bishops were debating among themselves about the Equal Rights Amendment, changing their positions from support, to rejection, to neutrality because of the question of abortion, 70% of American Catholics went ahead to endorse ERA without reference to the controversy going on among their bishops.[10]

American Catholics Are Americans and Catholics

But a culture that is based on individual freedom is not the only significant influence on how Americans and American Catholics look at religion. Our life experiences take place in an environment very much influenced, if not actually controlled, by economic realities and political practicalities. We live in a world limited by what is "the possible" for us, and frequently the choices we have are not between good and evil, but choices between evils. While Catholics recognize that the clergy, pope, bishops and priests, may speak on public issues, "When the issue gets closer to something the individual perceives is within grasp, he or she is more likely to label it a matter of individual conscience."[11]

> When church leaders exercise their teaching authority on political or social questions, they will often receive a polite reception from American Catholic parishioners. Nevertheless, the closer the teaching gets to personal morality, the less authority the people accord to it.[12]

Sociologist Dean Hoge points out that all people, unless bad health intervenes, make their decisions based on the needs of their families, their careers and their life-styles, and in that order.[13]

In addition, medical advances, scientific progress and technological development have brought enormous benefits to the American people. Eradication of some diseases, worldwide instant communication, good transportation, democracy and stable elected government, peace, and the mitigating of poverty, hunger and oppression have made possible new ways of acting that could only be dreamed about in the past. All of these advances in living have enabled Americans to develop their distinctive national life-style, "the American way of life." Its allure has drawn and continues to draw millions of immigrants from all nations and races of the world. In spite of its deficiencies, millions of people are convinced that the "American way" is "the best way" to live.

At the same time, the very advances that have made the American way of life bring with them a host of new problems, especially for those who seek to live out the gospel teachings.

Archbishop John R. Quinn listed some of these "critical new realities" when he addressed Pope John Paul II as one of the spokesmen for the American hierarchy in their meeting with him in California on September 16, 1987.

1. The fact that the United States is a major military power in the world.
2. Pervasive divorce and family instability, which so greatly harm the ability of the family to be the basic transmission belt of civilization and religion.
3. The immensely high standard of living enjoyed by a great part of American society and the responsibilities as well as the human problems this standard of living creates.
4. The development of new medical technologies which aid in both the generation and the prolongation of life, and the shocking paradox that the noble profession of medicine, the servant of human life and well-being, has also become a destroyer of human life through widespread abortion.
5. The constantly developing insights of the psychological and sociological sciences into the nature of human sexuality and of the human emotional life.
6. The sexual revolution, which has created a permissive climate in which sexual activity is declared to have a

value independent of other human responsibilities and moral exigencies.

7. The dramatically altered and changing social status of women, with its concomitant impact on personal meaning and identity.

8. The increased, widespread high level of education among American Catholics and its impact on their understanding of and expectations about their role in the church.[14]

In 1987 Catholics Wished To Remain Catholics

In spite of the many cultural and social factors that might seem to lessen Catholics' attachment to their church, in 1987 they wished to remain Catholic. George Gallup wrote:

> The picture of American Catholics that emerges from our data is that of a group of people secure in their sense of identity as Catholics. In some ways, they are extremely upbeat; in other areas, they have some serious criticisms of the church and some serious disagreements with church teaching. But neither criticisms nor disagreements have changed their sense of belonging to the church, indeed their sense of ownership of the church. They believe that their criticism will eventually be heard, partly because they have institutionalized a sense of change. They don't even necessarily want the church to change all of its teachings with which they disagree; they just want those teachings viewed as ideals which may seem impractical in the real world and from which they may dissent in conscience.[15]

Andrew M. Greeley, another respected if more controversial sociologist, basically confirmed Gallup's analysis. Writing in 1987, he saw the membership in the church as having stabilized since 1975 in spite of the changes in the church after the Second Vatican Council, the pope's teachings, and "strange doctrines and practices [the people] encounter in many parishes and dioceses." He wrote:

> If there is one fact that seems incontrovertible to me after almost three decades of research on American Catholicism, it is that the laity in the United States have reacted to the changes and the traumas of the last quarter-century with astonishing tranquility.[16]

He went on to note that the proportion of those who had left the church was about the same in 1985 as it was in 1960, 13%, and 87% still attended Mass on at least some Sundays of the year. In addition, contrary to a popularly accepted misconception, the 1987 rate of departure from and return to church practice was statistically the same as it had been in the past, and it was a statistic based not on social change but on age.

Statistics reveal the following about young people:

> [They] are less likely to vote, to affiliate with a political party, to make a definitive career choice, to choose a permanent sexual partner and to stay in a particular job. As they grow older—not much older—they make choices in all these matters.

Furthermore, all drift back to the church at around the same age, regardless of marital status and whether or not they have children.[17]

Gallup concluded from his statistical evidence that, far from being in a state of decline, the Catholic Church was healthy. Indeed, "American Catholics are in the middle of a religious revival."

He cites three indicators: (1) "a significant increase in Catholic religious activity outside Mass in the past decade"; (2) "the increase in such activity among young Catholics [which] has paralleled the increase among all Catholics"; and (3) the dramatic increase of the reading of scripture, while the frequency of prayer, confession and the recitation of the rosary has remained constant since the early 1970s.[18]

There Have Been Significant Changes from 1987 to 1993

Dean Hoge reports:

Stated most generally, the trends [comparing results of 1987 and 1993] indicate a shift from reliance by Catholics on institutional church authority to individual authority with regard to moral questions.[19]

For example, since 1987 there has been a 17% increase in the number of Catholics saying you can be a good Catholic without obeying the church's teaching on abortion: 39% in 1987, 56% in 1993. In 1987, 66% of Catholics said you could be a good Catholic without obeying the church 's teaching on birth control; in 1993 this increased to 73%.

Mass attendance on the other hand has remained virtually unchanged: 44% went to Mass at least weekly in 1987, 43% in 1993.

At the same time, Hoge points out there are warning signals: "Our data lead us to expect a gradual shift from specific Catholic identity to a broader Christian identity, so that young people will have more and more difficulty feeling a unique truth and value in the Roman Catholic Church."[20]

Hoge's colleague in this poll, Jim Davidson, observes that there is a growing generation gap, with the youngest being identified as those between the ages of 18-34. He says:

The youngest generation is the most experiential and individualistic in its faith orientation. It is relatively detached from the institutional church and the least well informed of the three generations.[21]

Nevertheless, the church does seem to remain healthy as Gallup reported in 1987. David O'Brien, a third collaborator in the most recent poll, concludes:

> The basic pattern of post-Vatican II American Catholicism...remains intact; renewal is strong, reform lags far behind. People love Jesus and take the gospel seriously—major goals of renewal. They make their own choices. It is far from clear they make the wrong choices all that often.[22]

Faith Brings Joy and Peace to Moral Living

Given the basic vibrant health of the Catholic Church in the United States, what can be done to assure its continued vigor? The church needs to communicate the traditional moral norms of the church universal (Catholic) in a positive, attractive and winning way so that Catholics today can achieve the end for which they were created: peace and happiness. In short, the church needs to communicate Catholic spirituality, especially sexual morality, as the good news of salvation.

In times past, when there was not the extensive theological pluralism that permeates contemporary Catholicism today, the task of communicating right from wrong was relatively simple. When all was said and done, most Catholics, both lay and ordained, agreed upon the basic norms of Catholic morality.

That is no longer the case. The Dutch Dominican theologian, Edward Schillebeeckx, offers a helpful explanation:

> In a pluralistic society even the personality structure of belief has changed in modern men and women....[The] multiplicity of possibilities [of choice in the modern world] has also become an internal qualification of a person's conviction about life. This multiplicity does not lie "outside" a person as an open market place but is internalized throughout human consciousness....Modern

believers know that there is also truth in other convictions about life.[23]

Yet Catholics can assent to the teaching of the church, as that teaching is the interpretation of divine revelation, only insofar as they have faith. In his meeting with the bishops in San Francisco, Pope John Paul II said:

> The church is a community of faith. To accept faith is to give assent to the word of God as transmitted by the church's authentic magisterium. Such assent constitutes the basic attitude of the believer and is an act of the will as well as of the mind. It would be altogether out of place to try to model this act of religion on attitudes drawn from secular culture.[24]

Without the kind of faith of which the pope speaks, then, Catholics, including sincere Catholics, frequently do not see any connection between the moral demands of the gospel and the joy, peace and inner harmony that enable Catholics to live together in the unity of love in family, parish and society. Yet it is precisely this life of practical, mature faith, the foundation of both a personal and parish spirituality that gives us the power to be "the light of the world" and the "salt of the earth" (Mt 5:13-14), and allows the church to be a "sign lifted up among the Gentiles."

A Lack of Good News Causes Confusion

If faith gives Catholics the power to assent to the teachings of the Gospel as transmitted through the centuries by the preaching of the church, the reason so many Catholics reject some church teachings today is not lack of faith; it is because they do not see how these particular teachings of the church relate to the gospel. Since the vast majority do not read the scriptures or study church documents or even read diocesan newspapers, they depend on the parish leaders, and if these do not connect the church and the gospel, Catholics will not see the church teachings as leading to the gospel joy they hunger for.

All too often Catholics do not realize that what the church teaches, it teaches precisely to bring peace and joy to believers in Jesus Christ in all aspects of their lives. Hence, the good news needs communicators who proclaim the truth of God's saving action as passed on in the Catholic church in ways that can be effectively embraced by the people of God through faith.

When he addressed the pope at his meeting with the bishops in San Francisco, Archbishop John R. Quinn said:

> We [bishops] regard [negative criticism of the church's moral teaching] as a continuing incentive to search more carefully for more effective ways of translating the church's teaching into more attractive language—even when presenting the difficult or corrective teachings of the gospel—so that "in language intelligible to each generation, [the church] can respond to the perennial questions that men ask" (*Gaudium et Spes,* 4).[25]

"Must" Preaching Does Not Deepen Faith

So often, Sunday homilists preach the moral injunctions of the gospel and the parables that give rise to them as a series of "musts." If the listeners obey the "musts," they will win a heavenly reward; if not, they will be condemned.

The problem is that frequently the Sunday "musts" are so difficult to achieve that people hear them only as unrealistic ideals quite unconnected with the reality of daily life. They may be desirable ideals, and people may actually wish they could live that way, but since the listeners do not experience within themselves the power to live according to those ideals, the moral injunctions remain just that: unattainable ideals.

Today, for example, large numbers of young, sexually active and fertile couples struggle with the high cost of living, compete fiercely for career advancement or just to hang on to their jobs, and endure great stress as they try to raise their children to be able to live successfully in today's society.

At the same time, the need of married couples for sexual relations with one another—which, after all, is a gift from God—remains. They hunger to express their love for one another sexually—again, a gift from God. The only way many experience having the power to satisfy that deep-seated natural appetite and, at the same time, avoid having children which they feel they cannot raise properly is to use artificial birth control.

Since "must" preaching does not give the listener the sense of power necessary to obey, but simply affirms the necessity of doing so, the "sinner" is left in a morass of guilt and frustration with his or her own weakness. Furthermore, since no one can live long in a state of depression, Catholics who are unable to live in conformity with the norms they hear apodictically proclaimed simply deny the objective immorality of the act and the authority of anyone to say that the act is objectively immoral. So we have the rather common phenomenon of good Catholics selecting those teachings of the church which they find compatible with their experience of life and rejecting the others.

Even Preaching on Morality Should Move the Heart

The preacher, meanwhile, feels fulfilled because he is satisfied that he has "proclaimed the word of God," and if the people won't accept it, he is not to blame. The guilt is on the listener.

Today, given the values of our American culture, when the preacher warns his listeners, he cannot just "proclaim" the bare, unadorned truth—a catechism proposition or a terse

axiom of moral theology. Week after week, preachers, catechists, evangelists and parents have the responsibility of finding those words, phrases, stories and images that both
enlighten the mind and move the heart.

Pope John Paul II said, again speaking to the bishops:

> The way to the heart very often passes through the
> mind, and throughout the length and breadth of the
> church there is need today for a new effort of evange-
> lization and catechesis directed to the mind.
> Elsewhere I have mentioned the relationship between
> the gospel and culture. Here I wish to underline the
> importance of the formation of the mind at every level
> of Catholic life.[26]

To bring about that conversion of mind as well as of
heart, there is an urgent necessity for the parish team to
explore more deeply and explain more fully the reasons
behind the moral injunctions of the gospel and, therefore, of
the church. In this way, they can effectively demonstrate to
their contemporaries just how moral living enables believers
to penetrate more deeply into the mystery of the divine and,
in union or *communio* with that mystery, find growth in holiness and happiness.[27]

The communication of morals is effective when it reveals
the transcendent goodness, wisdom and power of God, which
are then incarnated into the particularity of time and space by
those who are united to him through faith in Jesus Christ and
the love of the Holy Spirit.

The Essence of God Is Holiness

Human beings, Genesis 1:27 tells us, were made in the
image and likeness of God. The essence of God is holiness
(*CCC* 2809).[28] That is, God is totally above all of his creatures; all power, all wisdom, are God's. God is completely

apart from everything else, infinitely above everything—transcendent. God is an infinitely creative energy, a mysterious life-giving force. Still, for all God's internal perfection—the life of the Trinity—God is other-directed. God reaches beyond himself to the things he has made. God's love orders all things according to God's all-knowing, infallible plan (*CCC* 306). God's glory is precisely his holiness as it shines forth into the world, and especially as it shapes the chosen people. Before God's perfect holiness everything created can only stand in silent awe.

Because of the limitations of human language, these abstract words cannot adequately communicate the reality of God's holiness they are meant to represent. Nevertheless, since holiness is the primary characteristic of the divine, we who are made in God's own image are meant to reflect God's own holiness. So, being like God means being holy. "The temple of God is holy; and you are that temple" (1 Cor 3:17).

Because all human beings are made in the image and likeness of God, all human beings have an innate longing to share in God's holiness. It is intrinsic to our nature. As Saint Augustine wrote in his Confessions, "Our hearts are restless until they rest in Thee." Whether or not one is a believer, our good actions as judged by human reason itself will lead each person to reflect to some degree God's holiness in his or her life.

But God wanted more for his chosen people. For this reason, God inspired the writing of the sacred scriptures to reveal his holiness and to show human beings a more certain way to become holy like God. Nowhere in scripture is the way to holiness revealed more perfectly than in Jesus Christ, who is the "way, the truth and the life" (Jn 14:16). When we see Jesus, we see the Father (Jn 14:9). By uniting ourselves with Jesus, we achieve the glorious holiness of God himself (cf. Col 3:1-17).

Holiness Leads to the Imaging of God

To image God as his chosen ones, therefore, believers have to become holy. When the Letter to the Ephesians sums up all of God's gifts to his chosen people, it begins with the gift of holiness, being like God himself who chose us in Christ before the foundation of the world to be holy and without blemish before him (Eph 1:4).

Our faith-enlightened reason impels us to act in a way which is consonant with the holiness of God, since by faith we are being "transformed into the same image from glory to glory as from the Lord who is Spirit" (2 Cor 3:18).

The reason so many Catholics have difficulty accepting church teaching today about morality is that all too often parish leaders do not adequately stress becoming holy as God is holy as the norm for human actions. All our free choices are made with an end in view, either proximate or ultimate. All our good actions are good precisely because they achieve an end which leads us to participate more fully in the holiness of God. When we act in opposition to God's holiness, we sin. Indeed, it is impossible to define sin apart from a consideration of the holiness of God. As the psalmist says, "Against you alone have I sinned" (Ps 51:4).

The "Original Sin" Was To Deny God's Holiness

The opposition of sin to God's holiness was established in the third chapter of the Book of Genesis in the story of the fall of the first man and woman.[29] Ultimately their "sin" was their failure to acknowledge the utter transcendence and holiness of God by seeking to become like him, not through obedience to his will, but by the eating of the forbidden fruit (*CCC* 397–398).[30] This was the primordial rebellion, the root of all subsequent "sin."

With this act, the human creatures turned their focus from the glory of the immortal, holy God to themselves, and immediately they perceived themselves as they really were — finite, weak, shameful, naked. And so, conscious of their unholiness, they hid themselves from the Holy One.

Centuries later, Peter recapitulates this incident when he confronts for the first time the Holy One of God, Jesus. He cries out immediately, "Depart from me, O Lord, for I am a sinful man."

As we grow in holiness that growth of itself makes us more sensitive to the evil—sin—within us; this is a great blessing because without sensitivity to sin, we will not be able to perceive what is blocking our union with God. Sin blinds us to God's holiness. In fact, the Letter to the Romans (Rom 1:18-32) cites our failure to recognize God's "invisible attributes of eternal power and divinity" as the actual cause of God's wrath on the human race. The "wrath" results in blindness of both heart and mind, in spite of the fact that God's holiness is "able to be understood and perceived in what he has made." This blindness of heart and mind in turn leads to all kinds of reprehensible human actions such as sexual perversion, lust, greed, and murder.

The list of evils Paul enumerates as resulting from spiritual blindness is both long and exhaustive, with sexual disorders being a major effect vividly described in verses 24-28. But whatever the evil, all flow from the "impiety and wickedness of those who suppress the truth by their wickedness" (v. 18).

Yet, there is an immediate difficulty for the parish formation team today, because our contemporary American understanding of right and wrong, which is a necessary ingredient in our struggle for holiness, is greatly influenced, if not predominantly shaped, by secular values. Therefore Paul cautions Christians about the standards we apply in communicating morality, because God in his wisdom did not want human beings to be able to come to him except through faith. Because God's wisdom is so opposed to the wisdom of the world, they crucified Jesus, the Lord of glory. Thus Paul sums up his preaching of the mystery: we teach what scripture calls "the things that no eye has seen and no ear has heard, things beyond the mind of man, all that God has prepared for those who love him" (cf. 1 Cor 1:21; 2:7-9).

By frankly acknowledging that the fullness of human life and the rewards of living according to the mind of our creator are dependent on the revelation of his holiness, the parish team can ground its communication of good news spirituality on the highest and most secure of bases—the holiness of God himself.

2

The Holiness of God

*I*n story after story, especially in the Old Testament but also in the New, the sacred writers reveal the holiness of God: God's unique transcendence, intelligence, love and power. The word "holiness" and its cognates appear 565 times in the Bible. The New Testament writers greatly expand the concept of God's holiness by presenting holiness as an attribute we can share through the power of the Holy Spirit. In his Sermon on the Mount, presented by the evangelist Matthew as the inaugural address of the New Moses to his chosen people, Jesus described how he was bringing to perfection the teaching of the Old Law (cf. Mt 5:20-48). By the time Jesus finished his exposition of the spirit behind the Mosaic legislation, his listeners were vividly conscious of the perfection of holiness to which Jesus was calling them: "Be perfect as your heavenly Father is perfect" (Mt 5:48).

There is a popular notion today that God wants us to be well and healthy—whole instead of holy. Yet most who seek miraculous cures remain ill; the crippled remain crippled; the dying die. If health and wholeness were the goal of life, none of these would achieve it, and frustration would be the greatest suffering.

But the good news of the gospel is that all the uncured ill can be holy; all the crippled can be holy; all the dying can die holy. And when they are holy, they are at peace. In other words, being holy is being whole in the most perfect sense of the term.

Since the goal of effective moral preaching is to guide the faithful into imaging the holiness of God, the parish team needs to recapture for their listeners the sense of awe and wonder that permeates the Bible.

The Holiness of God Gets Things Started

The holiness of God begins to be revealed as an intimate constituent of human life when in chapter 12 of Genesis, without warning, the Lord God speaks to Abram.[1] The text uses the divine name first revealed to Moses (cf. Ex 6:3), "Yahweh."[2] It is here that revelation leaves the obscure shadows of myth and enters into history.

> The Lord said to Abram: "I will make you a great nation, and I will bless you" (Gen 12:1-3).

What is striking about this story is that it starts so abruptly. God simply speaks, and he speaks a blessing. For no discernible reason, he chose to manifest himself to an unknown nomad living in a society that worshiped a number of pagan gods. Scripture does not attribute to Abram any particular virtue. It gives only his genealogy as son of Terah, who had previously left Ur and migrated to Haran. Ur was located at the heart of an ancient and highly developed civilization, whose religious traditions seemed to have influenced the biblical traditions themselves—the imagery used in the creation myths and the story of the flood, for example.

But when Yahweh speaks to Abram, we immediately encounter a significant departure from the legends of the gods current in the Mesopotamian region. When God spoke to Abram, he did not insist on service from him or demand worship with the threat of punishment if he failed to do so. Rather, when Yahweh spoke it was to confer a blessing. Scripture emphasizes that "Abram went as the Lord directed him" (Gen 12:4).

The Lord's generosity to Abram is confirmed one night in a mysterious covenant ceremony that fills Abram with terror. Abram had sacrificed some animals by God's instructions. When he split them up, he made them into a kind of corridor and then fell into a trance. Late that night, a flaming torch passed down the corridor between the halves, and scripture says that God made a covenant with Abram (Gen 15:17-18).

The relations between the Lord and Abram are characterized by the Lord's continually blessing Abram and by Abram's unquestioning obedience to the Lord. Paul is later to note that Abraham's faith was the source of his righteousness (Rom 4:1-3).

After God had renewed his promises to Abraham a number of times (God gave him this new name in Genesis 17:5), he tests Abraham's faith by asking him to sacrifice his only son Isaac, the son of God's promises. Again unquestioningly, Abraham prepares to sacrifice Isaac, but God stops him at the last moment, saying:

> I know now that you are devoted to God...not withholding your beloved son from me. I will bless you abundantly (Gen 22:12-18).

In the story of Abraham we have the first unfolding of the holiness of God in the context of lived history. Chapters 1-11 identify the person who speaks to Abraham; he is the God who created the universe and everything in it and did so without effort and according to a rational plan that was meant to be a blessing to all his beloved creatures, but especially human beings.

But now God speaks and makes a promise to Abraham on the strength of his own name, his own holiness. At the same time, we find the first of a series in a theme that will underlie the entire scriptures. Trusting obedience is the proper response to God's holiness and the key to both reward and punishment. God is always faithful to his promise of blessing, but as the prophets of the Old Testament will point out, if the holiness of God is violated by disobedience, the violator will be subject to fearful punishments.

From the story of God's call to Abram, we learn a fundamental characteristic of God's holiness: it starts things. It gets things moving and keeps them moving. God himself begins the communication of his own holiness to Abraham and through him to all humankind without reference to the merits of human beings. God acts sovereignly, freely, simply because he wishes to do so. From the beginning, he seeks to share his own holiness, and he has the power to do so. All the events that happen to us, therefore, are part of God's working out his purpose in his time and in his own way. And the end result will be what God wills.[3]

After Abraham, the theme of God's holiness is somewhat obscured in the patriarchal histories. It does not become clearly evident again until the call of Moses to lead his people out of Egypt.

Exodus Emphasizes God's Holiness

Like Abraham, Moses is an unlikely candidate for a conversation with God. He is a murderer fleeing for his life from the Egyptian court. Having attained refuge tending sheep, Moses notices the unusual sight of a bush on fire but not consumed. When he walks over to examine the phenomenon more closely, God speaks from the midst of the burning bush. He instructs Moses to remove his sandals, "for the place where you stand is holy ground." Then God reveals himself as the God of Abraham, the God of Isaac, and the God of Jacob.

When he hears that it is God who is speaking to him, Moses is overcome with fear (Ex 3:5-6).

Then God tells Moses how he has heard the cries of his people and, faithful to his promises to the patriarchs, he will deliver them from the oppression and slavery of the Egyptians In addition, he has chosen Moses to be the instrument by which he shall accomplish his purpose. "I shall show my power and strike Egypt with all the wonders I am going to work there" (Ex 3:20).

Moses, on the other hand, has grave misgivings. He feels particularly unsuited to the mission he is being given because he is "slow of speech and tongue." He is, in fact, so reluctant to obey that the Lord becomes angry with Moses. At the burning bush, God is like a loving father with a child still full of fear for the unknown. Sometimes a father has to give the command to step out in rather strong terms to overcome the child's fear, and, loving Father that he is, God helps Moses speak by giving him his brother Aaron to work with him. God says to Moses, "I shall help you to speak and Aaron too, and I will instruct you both in what to do" (Ex 4:15).[4]

When Moses and Aaron appear before Pharaoh, he is adamant in refusing to release the Hebrews from their servitude, and indeed increases their burdens. This reaction sets the scene for a series of prodigious events that manifest the power of God. These prodigies, the last of which is the slaying of the first-born of the Egyptians, lead up to the Israelites' crossing the Red Sea which has become dry land, while their Egyptian pursuers are drowned in the returning waters.

Exodus 15:1-18 contains one of the oldest poems in the Bible, dating back to the thirteenth century B.C.[5] It celebrates God's victory over the Egyptians, and it opens with a refrain that praises God's glory:

> I sing to the Lord: he has covered himself with glory;
> horse and rider he has thrown into the sea (v. 1).

Verse 11 praises God's holiness and the holiness of the land to which he is leading them, revealing both the powerful nature of God's holiness and the fact that God is merciful to his people.

Holiness in the People is the Response to God's Holiness

During their trek in the Desert of Sin, having successfully escaped from the Egyptians, the Israelites were miraculously fed quail and manna. This latter was to be collected every day except the Sabbath because that was a complete day of rest in honor of the Lord (Ex 16:25). By this observance, an ancient one, the people were kept constantly aware of God's presence in their midst and conscious of his guidance and protection.

These experiences and those of miraculous feedings in the desert culminate when God reveals himself in all his majesty and holiness on Mount Sinai (Horeb in Deuteronomy) and concludes a covenant with this people in which he promises them his protection if they will obey his commandments.

Before Moses received the covenant on Mount Sinai, the people were warned by Moses to sanctify themselves and wash their garments. He said to them: "Be ready for the third day. Have no intercourse with any woman" (Ex 19:15). Here begins the demand for holiness in the people as an acknowledgment of God's holiness.

The Lord's theophany on Sinai was accompanied by lightning, a heavy cloud, smoke, and a trumpet blast. When God spoke to Moses it sounded like thunder to the people. God's holiness is glorious—so glorious it causes awe and terror. In fact, they were so terrified by God's power that they could not even listen to him for fear they would die. Therefore

Moses reassured them, saying that God appeared to them like that so they would keep themselves from sin (Ez 20:18-20).

This is a splendid story to read through children's eyes. Children are still open to the marvels beyond everyday life; their imaginations respond to the vivid images that fill the Old Testament. The Israelites were like children, so God taught them just as we teach little children today. Where we can only read about great theophanies, the Israelites had the privilege of seeing them and being changed by them.

Legal Prescriptions Flow from God's Holiness

After the awe-inspiring manifestation of the divine holiness, Moses relays by way of the Commandments how the chosen people should live in order to reflect God's holiness which they had just witnessed. In addition to the Ten Commandments (Ex 20:1-17) there are laws regarding the treatment of slaves, personal injury, damage of property, theft, trusts, and loans as well as laws regarding religious observances (Ex 20-40).

Of particular importance in maintaining the sense of identity as a people uniquely dedicated to God and holy in his sight is the legislation regarding the observance of the Sabbath. It is a day which is to be considered holy—set apart—from all other days. No work was to be done by anyone, even by a non-Israelite living with the people. In keeping the Sabbath, the Israelites were constantly reminded that their God created the heavens and the earth in six days, and rested on the seventh. The Sabbath, then, was a way of keeping the people faithful to Yahweh, even though they were surrounded by pagans. Consequently, Sabbath observance was strictly enforced, and one of the major charges brought against Jesus was that he violated the Sabbath. The law regarding the Sabbath is one of the

Ten Commandments and is accompanied by a rather long explanation of the legislation (Ex 20:8-11).[6]

The remainder of the Pentateuch, Leviticus and Deuteronomy in particular, gives extensive legislation regarding every aspect of Hebrew life, all of which was intended to mold the Israelites into a holy people that would make the name of God holy by reflecting God's holiness in their own lives. Even the food they ate not only nourished their bodies, it was also a reminder that they were God's holy people and, therefore, had to avoid certain foods that were considered "unclean."[7]

Some of the regulations seem unreasonably severe to modern minds for two reasons. First, our lives in the United States are the result of centuries of civilizing activity. In comparison with the Israelites our lives are comfortable, safe, and marked by mutual respect. In other parts of the world, we see great violence and cruelty—much of it exercised in "just" punishments of evildoers—like amputations and torture. Some countries today still have forms of slavery. The Israelites also had a hard and primitive life; they were treated cruelly by their enemies and they responded in kind. As a result of the hardship of those times and cultures, they had learned to expect severe punishment.

The second reason the regulations seem unreasonable is that they were made to build up the community precisely as a community. Whereas we have become very much shaped by our culture to be individuals whose happiness depends on our personal success, happiness for the Israelites could only occur in the context of their life as members of the community of God's chosen people. Today we might call these severe ceremonial regulations effective methods of "behavior modification" to help members become more fully integrated into community values one of which was a graphic sense of God's holiness acknowledged by awe. The ceremonial laws had rigid penalties attached to their violation. In some cases the penalty was death. For example, Aaron and his sons were to wear linen shorts under their tunics "to cover their nakedness from loin to thigh" when they entered the tent of meeting or approached the altar, "lest they incur guilt and die" (Ex 28:43).

In fact, Aaron's sons Nadab and Abihu did die for a ritual violation which seems quite minor: they offered incense to God that he had not authorized. God sent down fire upon them that consumed them (Lv 10:1-3). But their deaths certainly teach that God's holiness is to be reverenced, and punishment for violation of God's holiness was quick and severe; the two offenders were buried outside the camp without customary mourning rites.

All of these incidents illustrate the importance attached to the command given to the entire Israelite community by Moses, when God said to him: "Speak to the whole Israelite community and tell them: Be holy, for I, the Lord your God, am holy. Revere your mother and father, and keep my Sabbaths. I, the Lord, am your God" (Lv 19:2-3). Even respect for the aged was a reflection of God's holiness in his people:

> Rise in the presence of the elderly, and show respect for
> the old; thus shall you fear your God. I am the Lord (Lv
> 19:32).

God's Holiness Provides for the Needs of God's People

Moses is the greatest of the prophets because he spoke face to face with God; he is the acknowledged founder of the Israelite nation through his exceptional leadership and legislative ability. Yet the great Moses himself was severely punished by God: he was not permitted to enter the land to which he was leading his people because he "was not faithful in showing forth God's holiness before the Israelites" (Num 20:12).

Scholars have long sought to identify the exact nature of the sin of Moses; it is not clear in the text because of the brevity with which it is recorded. *The Jerome Biblical Commentary* explains it best perhaps because it is true to the spirit of the Book of Numbers which is so conscious of manifesting the divine holiness. God commanded Moses to manifest God's mercy by striking the rock, and then water would gush forth. Moses, however, twisted this show of God's power and mercy by chastising the people for their lack of faith. Instead of a joyful exhibit of God's holiness in his love for his people, Moses showed anger. In the biblical phrase of Numbers 20:12, they had failed to "show forth my sanctity," i.e., to glorify and hallow God's name before the people.[8]

In those primitive days, failure to acknowledge God's holiness is severely punished frequently in scripture. For example, the wandering in the desert for forty years immediately after the exodus from Egypt was to punish those Israelites who denied the Lord's glory, a radiation of God's transcendent holiness on earth (Num 14:21-23).

The mysterious death of Uzziah (1 Chr 13:9-12) for doing the good work of steadying the ark of the covenant makes sense only when the reader understands the immense holiness of God that was violated by such a profane touch. So fearful was Uzziah's death to the great King David that David refused to bring the ark of the covenant with him; only when it became evident that the ark was a blessing for the people and not a curse did David have the ark moved to Jerusalem, and then David himself danced before it in the triumphal procession (1 Chr 15).

The Prophets Proclaim God's Holiness

The prophet Isaiah preached in eighth-century Judah during a time of moral corruption, political tension and foreign invasion. During his lifetime, the Northern Kingdom fell to the

Assyrians, never to rise again, and those victorious armies even reached into Judah. In the north, Amos inveighed against the same evils that were rampant in Judah, but to no avail.

The Bible sees the fall of the Northern Kingdom as God's punishment for its sin. In the Old Testament, the writers skip over the secondary causes because they want to focus on God and his creative actions in the world. Nevertheless, modern readers, with more sophisticated tools of interpretation available to us, can easily see that it was the moral corruption of the people that left them weakened and unable to resist the onslaught of their foes. Luxuries had weakened their bodies, greed their wills so that when the moment of crisis came, they did not have the resources or the will to fight to win. This is what is behind the teaching of the Bible that since they failed to repent of their offenses against God's holiness, the Northern Kingdom was conquered by God's agents of destruction—the Assyrians.

One of the most vivid descriptions of God's holiness is found in Isaiah's vision of God when he is first called to the prophetic ministry. He sees God seated on a lofty throne attended by angels. "'Holy, holy, holy is the Lord of hosts!' they cried one to the other. 'All the earth is filled with his glory!' At the sound of that cry, the frame of the door shook and the house was filled with smoke." Isaiah thought he was doomed because he knew himself to be unclean. "Then one of the seraphim flew to me, holding an ember which he had taken with tongs from the altar. He touched my mouth with it. 'See,' he said, 'now that this has touched your lips, your wickedness is removed, your sin purged'" (Is 6:1–7).

Filled, therefore, with a profound sense of God's holiness from his own experience of the call to prophesy, Isaiah warned the people that God's holiness would be vindicated by the manifestation of his just judgment against evil-doers, in this case the kingdom of Judah itself (Is 5:16,25).

Because Judah failed to repent (that is, change its life-style to image the holiness of God), in the summer of 587 B.C.

proud Jerusalem, the capital city of Judah, fell to the Babylonian conquerors. Then, and again in 582/581, the leading and most skilled craftsmen of Judah were deported to Babylon where they remained until the Edict of Cyrus in 538 allowed the exiles to return to Jerusalem. This tragic period marks a definitive change in the nature of Judaism; it could no longer revolve around Temple worship, but depended solely upon its devotion to God's Law.

The prophet Ezekiel saw the punishments of the exiles as due to the "abominations" of Judah, the idolatry into which the people had fallen which was so opposed to God's holiness. Nevertheless, God did not abandon his people. Rather Ezekiel saw fantastic, powerful, moving visions of God's glory leaving the Temple in Jerusalem and going to be with the exiles in Babylon. In spite of their sins, God's holiness abided with his people.

The Book of Ezekiel opens with his famous vision of the "chariot of Yahweh" on the banks of the river Chebar in Babylon (cf. Ez 1:4-28). It records another fantastic vision of Ezekiel in which he sees God's holiness leaving the city to rest on a mountain nearby (Ez 10:19). At the end of the book, Ezekiel has a glorious vision of the new Temple which will be constructed in the restored city of Jerusalem after the Jews return from their exile.

The terrible "punishment" of the exile led to an even greater blessing. As a result of the exile, God shaped the Jews to be the people to whom God would send the Messiah, Jesus Christ. Because of the exile, you and I are able to be members of God's new people, the church of Jesus Christ.

Holiness Leads to Evangelization

Moreover, with Ezekiel there is a new dimension to the holiness of God. It is not a holiness meant simply to inspire awe and respect among the Israelites. The centuries leading up to the exile stressed that aspect, although, in the long run, fear alone was inadequate to prevent the people's rebellion.

Ezekiel stresses that God's holiness is to be made manifest beyond Israel to the whole world when God rescues his people from their captivity in the country of their enemies and brings them back to their own land. The whole world will learn of God's power when Israel's enemies are defeated. Furthermore, after their return, God will continue to reveal his holiness to them because he will pour out his Spirit on the house of Israel (Ez 39:27-29).

Holiness Gives New Life

Furthermore, God's holiness is not just God's transcendent power and majesty. The famous vision of the dry bones reveals that God's holiness gives his people, dead through their own sins, new life through the outpouring of his own spirit. In their defeat and seeming abandonment by God, Israel had been like dead men and dried-up bones; in their return from exile, the dry bones rose from the grave to a new life and became a large army filled with God's own spirit (Ez 37:11-14).

The effect of the spirit is a new heart, which in fact characterized the Jewish people after the exile and which forms the basis for the Christian understanding of the life of grace through Jesus Christ. "I shall give you a new heart, and put a new spirit in you. I shall put my spirit in you, and make you keep my laws and sincerely respect my observances" (Ez 36:23-38).

Ezekiel stands firmly in the prophetic tradition which understood God's holiness as identified with his love, compassion and mercy, despite the transgressions of the people. His prophecy recalls the prophet Hosea, who prophesied just before the fall of the Northern Kingdom to Assyria. In spite of their sins, God, the Holy One of Israel, will forgive them because of his great love. Because God is the Holy One, he has no wish to destroy; God punishes only to save (Hos 11:8,9).

After the return from exile, the priests of Zadok "who did their duty to me in the sanctuary when the Israelites strayed from me" are given the task of offering clean sacrifices and making the people holy by teaching them the rules and regulations of the renewed Judaism. They are to instruct the people in the difference between what is sacred and what is profane and to make them understand the difference between the clean and the unclean. The priests are also to be judges in disputes, and to interpret God's laws and ordinances, celebrate the feasts, and keep the Sabbath holy (Ez 44:23-24).

The lengthy Psalm 119 extols the new spirit of restoration when it praises the Law of the Lord, emphasizing the life-giving qualities of God's word:

> Guide me in the way of your commandments,
>   I delight in them.
> Turn my heart to your decrees
>   and away from greed.
> Turn my eyes from lingering on vanities
>   give me life by your word (Ps 119:35-38).

Ezekiel's new understanding of God's relation to his people is consonant with chapters 40-55 of the Book of Isaiah. The post-exilic relation will be based on the power of God's word. Here we have the laying of the foundations for the New Testament's understanding of God's holiness made flesh in Jesus Christ and incarnated in us throughout the centuries through the preaching of God's holy word. Christian tradition, of course, has always maintained the intimate connection between God's word and the sacraments.

God's Holy Word Consoles and Saves

The character of the writings in chapters 40–55 of the Book of Isaiah are so different from chapters 1–39 that scholars see them as the product of another prophet to whom they give the name Deutero-Isaiah or Second Isaiah.

First of all, he is no longer addressing the people of Jerusalem but the exiles in Babylon. He is no longer threatening his people with destruction and punishment; that has already taken place. Instead he seeks to console them with promises of God's saving actions.

Deutero-Isaiah emphasizes the power of God's word:

> Though the grass withers and the flower wilts,
>> the word of our God stands forever (Is 40:8).

God's word is so powerful that it creates what it wills, but it is always a saving creation, a creation that takes place for the good of the poor and lowly; it is a special creation of love for all those who put their trust in the Lord (Is 45:23–25).

The clearest expression of the exalted nature and power of God's word is found in the last chapter of the book where it is compared to life-giving water:

> For just as from the heavens the rain and snow come down
>> and do not return there till they have watered the earth,
>> making it fertile and fruitful,
> Giving seed to him who sows
> and bread to him who eats,
> so shall my word be that goes forth from my mouth;
>> it shall not return to me empty but shall do my will,
>> achieving the end for which I sent it (Is 55:8–11).

In Deutero-Isaiah, too, we find the famous songs of the Suffering Servant, the mysterious servant of the Lord whose sufferings would bring about the redemption of the people. In the original context, the servant is the nation of Israel,[9] but even among the Jews after the exile, the songs were seen as referring to the Messiah who was to come. Christian tradition identifies Jesus with the servant (cf. Acts 8:32-35).

Job Is in Awe of God's Holiness

The Book of Job is probably subsequent to the preaching of Ezekiel; it seems to be post-exilic in origin, which means that the new understanding of God's holiness serves as the basis for the books pondering the mystery of God's holiness. The Book of Job has a very contemporary flavor; indeed, it has served as the basis for an extremely popular play on Broadway by Archibald Macleish, *J.B.* The main issue of the book is: How can a good God cause, permit or allow the existence of evil and suffering in the world he created? The answer that four of Job's friends give is that suffering is the result of human sin. Since Job knows himself to be innocent, he knows that his sin cannot be the cause of his suffering.

There is no answer given in the text, which must be read in its entirety to appreciate the force of its reflections, other than the fact that God's ways are so far above the human that they cannot be questioned or understood. After all his complaints against the divine providence which allows such suffering as he is undergoing, the book concludes with Job's admitting to God that he really is not capable of understanding the mystery of God's actions. God is too powerful, his designs far exceed the limits of mere human thought. Because he has been so arrogant in challenging God, Job ends by asking for forgiveness. God obviously grants it, because everything is restored to Job that he previously possessed—and he is even richer and more honored than before his terrible trial (Job 42:2-6).

Wisdom Makes Known God's Holiness

Both Psalm 68 and Psalm 139 are poems which are songs of praise in honor of God's omnipotent and omniscient holiness. Other psalms also celebrate God's holiness.

So great is the understanding of the holiness of God that the Book of Proverbs says: "The beginning of wisdom is the fear of the Lord, and knowledge of the Holy One is understanding" (Prov 9:10). John Paul II in *Fides et Ratio* shows the contemporary validity of this principle in current philosophical endeavors when he writes, "[God's] transcendent sovereignty and provident love in the governance of the world reason must recognize."[10]

The Book of Wisdom is one of the last books of the Old Testament, having been written around 50 B.C. In a number of passages[11] the author, a sage of Israel, speaks of the wisdom of God as a manifestation of God's holiness, "an emanation of the glory of the All-Powerful...untarnished power of God's active power, image of his goodness" (cf. Wis 7:25-26). He makes two significant contributions to the development of revelation as the age of the Old Testament draws to a close.

First, he personifies Wisdom as something distinct from God, thus preparing the way for Jesus, the Wisdom of God made flesh. Secondly, having some acquaintance with Greek thought, he is able to offer a solution to the problem that had plagued Job: God in his love and mercy will give true justice to all human beings beyond the grave because the human being is imperishable and will live forever. At that time all the mysteries of seeming injustice will be unfolded when God shows love, justice and mercy to be one.

Holiness Is Made Visible in the New Testament

Since the purpose of the Incarnation, revealed in the New Testament, is to put God into more intimate and immediate contact with his beloved creatures, humankind, by enabling them to become his children through faith,[12] the New Testament refines the understanding of the holiness of God. Instead of emphasizing awesome theophanies surrounded by thunder, lightning and fire as on Mount Sinai, the New Testament writers stress that the holiness of God is made visible in a single human being, Jesus Christ.

In what may be an early Christian hymn, Paul describes Jesus as a cosmic figure who is the very image of God himself. Jesus was created first, and all other creations both visible and invisible, including the heavenly hosts, were created through him and for him (Col 1:15-16).

Jesus Is Holy with Divine Holiness

The holiness of Jesus is the foundation for his saving work. While the Letter to the Hebrews stresses that Jesus has become one with us in all things, except sin (cf. Heb 4:15-16), and, therefore, can offer himself as the perfect sacrifice on our behalf (cf. Heb 5:1-10), ultimately the efficacy of his sacrificial act is due to the fact, not that Jesus is human, but that he is divine and, therefore, holy, with the holiness of God himself. In the prologue to the Gospel of John, the writer describes how when the people looked upon Jesus, they saw his glory as the only Son of the Father. His teachings and his miracles were both signs that revealed God working in him (Jn 1:14, 18).

When the angel Gabriel announced Jesus' birth to Mary, he told her that the Holy Spirit would come upon her and the power of the Most High would overshadow her. As a result, she would conceive and bear a son. "The child will be holy and will be called Son of God" (Lk 1:31-36).

Faith Recognizes the Holiness of Jesus

Yet, although Christ is always holy with divine holiness, only men and women of faith can see his holiness. Paul says that the unbelievers are victims who have been so blinded by the god of this world that they cannot see the glory of Christ. They cannot see him as he really is—the image of God. It is as if a veil had been put over their eyes, the veil of unbelief that will lead them to ruin (2 Cor 4:3-4).

On the other hand, those called by the Father[13] recognize by faith the unique and overwhelming holiness of Jesus. At the beginning of his ministry, Jesus came to John to be baptized in the Jordan. Recognizing Jesus' holiness, John protested: "It is I who need baptism from you," he said, "and yet you come to me!" Nevertheless, at Jesus' insistence, John baptized him "and suddenly the heavens opened and he saw the Spirit of God descending like a dove and coming down on him. And a voice spoke from heaven, "This is my beloved Son in whom I am well pleased" (Mt 3:16-17).

Later, Peter upon first seeing Jesus recognizes his own unworthiness to appear before him: "Depart from me, Lord, for I am a sinful man" (Lk 5:8). In fact, the holiness of Jesus was so evident that even the devils acknowledged Jesus' holiness.[14] When Jesus cast out an unclean spirit from a possessed man, the devil left him, crying out: "I know who you are: the Holy One of God" (Mk 1:24).[15]

The Gospel of John has Jesus himself insisting that the Jews recognize his holiness; otherwise, "if you do not believe that I am he, you will die in your sins" (Jn 8:24). The gospel concludes Jesus' long argument with the Jews over his true identity with a solemn affirmation that enraged them because they regarded it as blasphemy. They realized that Jesus was asserting that he was divine when he said to them, "I tell you most solemnly, before Abraham was, I am."[16] Scripture goes on to say, "At this they picked up stones to throw at him; but Jesus hid himself and left the temple" (Jn 8:58).

Jesus Shares His Holiness

Just as sin cannot be fully known as sin without revelation, neither can the glory of holiness. This is particularly evident in the story of the passion in the Gospel of John. When his disciples feared Jesus' death on the cross as unjust punishment and humiliation, Jesus reveals that it is, in fact, his moment of glory. The revelation of Jesus' glory begins at the Last Supper when Judas leaves to betray him. From then on, all the horrific events of the passion and cross are borne by Jesus with more than heroic valor precisely to reveal God's compassionate love to a suffering and sinful world (Jn 13:31–32).

Moreover, the glory of Jesus was not something for Jesus alone. The whole purpose of his coming into the world was to share his glory with his faithful disciples (cf. Phil 2:6-11; Jn 17:21–23).

Jesus' understanding of sin and glory was rooted in the Old Testament. While he brought the teaching of Moses and the prophets to a new height of clarity and a new level of meaning, all of his teaching was built on the teaching of scripture already revealed to the chosen people. In his inaugural Sermon on the Mount in the Gospel of Matthew (Mt 5:1-7:29), and throughout his ministry, Jesus insisted on the lasting value of the Law and the Prophets. The whole purpose of Jesus' life was to bring the salvation God had started with the Israelites and the Jews to completion through faith in Jesus (Mt 5:17).

Nevertheless mere obedience to the Law is not enough to share his glory and the glory of his kingdom. Jesus demanded a change of heart. The scribes and Pharisees obeyed the law, but they did not have the virtue the law was designed to engender (Mt 5:20).

In the Sermon on the Mount, Jesus outlined the attitudes that are the foundation of his spiritual kingdom. The glory of the kingdom is the refulgence of the holiness of the human heart in union with the holiness of Jesus. Unless one is holy, one cannot appreciate or even understand the teachings of Jesus. Once, when Jesus got into an argument with his opponents about who he was, he said:

> Do you know why you cannot appreciate what I say? Because you are unable to understand my language. The devil is your father, and you prefer to do what your father wants (Jn 8:43-44).

Jesus' Holiness Allures Sinners

Three stories about Jesus in the gospels demonstrate how the evident holiness of Jesus was attractive to sinners and prompted them to turn back to the path of holiness.

In the Gospel of John Jesus kindly dismisses a woman taken "in the very act of adultery" with the simple statement, "Go, and do not sin again" (Jn 8:11).

In Luke 8:36-50, there is the touching, human story of a woman, evidently a rather well-known sinner in town, coming in to where Jesus was dining.

> She waited behind him crying, and her tears fell on his feet, and she wiped them away with her hair; then she covered his feet with kisses and anointed them with the perfume (Lk 8:38).

Although the Pharisees, those pillars of righteousness, disapproved of the entire display, Jesus graciously accepted her act of homage and sent her away "in peace."

Zacchaeus was a Jew who collected taxes for the Romans; he also defrauded his fellow Jews. Consequently, he was hated by them. Nevertheless, he too was attracted to Jesus—and

Jesus was attracted to him. At the end of their famous encounter in Luke 19:1-10, Zacchaeus renounces his former way of life. He gives away half his property to the poor and pays back to his victims four times the amount of which he had cheated them.

Paul sums up what God has done through the kindly holiness of Jesus when he writes to the Colossians:

> [God] has rescued us from the power of darkness [that is, all that is evil] and brought us to the kingdom of the Son that he loves, and in [the Son] we gain our freedom, the forgiveness of our sins (Col 1:13-14).

The Book of Revelation Gives Visions of Jesus' Glory

This divine holiness of Jesus is professed in a spectacular way by the writer of the Book of Revelation. The book starts with an overpowering vision of the risen Jesus as judge of the living and the dead (Rev 1:12-19), and then it goes on to say that even though the followers of Jesus are undergoing bloody persecution on earth, the heavenly courts are worshiping the holiness and glory of God and the risen Jesus whom the visionary sees as "the lamb who was slain."

The Book of Revelation was written during a time when the young Christian church was being persecuted by both Romans and Jews. The church was surrounded on all sides by enemies, and many of the faithful were becoming discouraged to the point of apostasy. Through the wonderful visions recounted in the book, the writer urges his readers to remain steadfast in the faith because after death, especially death by martyrdom, Jesus will be revealed in all his glory, and faithful Christians will be with him in his heavenly glory (Rev 4:2-3).

In this vision also, the heavenly courtiers sing "Holy, holy, holy is the Lord God Almighty." The countless number of heavenly hosts, "thousands and tens of thousands," cry out:

To the one who sits on the throne and to the lamb [the Risen Jesus] be praise and honor, glory and dominion, forever and ever (Rev 5:13).

Who would not want to be a part of that magnificent display of power, glory and, above all, divine holiness.

There Are Imprints of Holiness in Nature

God's power and majesty summed up in the term "transcendent holiness" put the Almighty God far above all his creatures. Yet only when Christians today joyfully acknowledge God's absolute dominion over all things can they appreciate the militant and aggressive qualities that are so shockingly evident in the reading of the Old Testament.

People who are close to nature and depend heavily upon the natural cycles of life and death, birth, growth and decay are more sensitive to seeing the imprint of the divine in natural events. Catastrophic storms, earthquakes, epidemics—all these are new lessons for the sensitive and religiously perceptive person on the power and grandeur of God.

These kinds of natural occurrences are used by the scriptural writers of the Old Testament to establish and communicate the holiness of God, but they also sensitize the Christian reader to discern the movements of grace in the New Testament era as well.

When the believer appreciates nature, he or she has no difficulty in seeing a further manifestation of the divine holiness in current affairs which constitute the political and social life of entire peoples. The Book of Wisdom consists of a series of reflections by a sage of Israel on God's holy power revealed in all events. Speaking to God, the wise man acknowledges that God governs all things with total justice. He punishes the guilty, yet does not punish the innocent. Precisely because

God is so powerful, he can afford to be lenient. His power enables him to be just (Wis 12:12-18).

The Lord God is the God of heavenly armies; angelic hosts do his every bidding. In the past, God sent forth the armies of Israel under his banner to take the land from the unbelievers so that God's true rule might be established firmly for his chosen people. Even today these images of God's holiness help us to put our trust in God

Since God is Lord of both the living and the dead, the death of every human being, especially the deaths of Christian martyrs, is an integral part of God's plan to manifest his holiness. The definitive revelation of the holiness of Jesus will take place when he destroys the enemy of us all—death.

> For he [Christ] must reign until he has put all his ene-
> mies under his feet, and the last enemy to be destroyed is
> death (1 Cor 15:25-26).

God Communicates His Holiness to His People

The New Testament, building on the holiness of God in the Old Testament while at the same time developing an awareness of the ontological holiness of Jesus, turns its attention to the communication of his holiness to those who believe in him. God spoke to Moses on Mount Sinai, calling him apart from the people to the mountain top, and then sending him back to the people with his words engraved in stone. This display of divine holiness was so graphic, terrifying and awe-inspiring that it formed the basis for the life of a whole nation and even today is a foundation of God's chosen people.

Although Jesus is the glory of the Father and the emanation of the holy luminescence of "The Other," "The Sacred," "The Mystery," Jesus proclaims his divine holiness not through earth-shaking prodigies of nature as on Mount Sinai, but through the manner of his death on the cross on Calvary.

> The centurion, who was standing in front of him, had seen how he had died, and he said, "In truth this man was the son of God" (Mk 15:39).[17]

The title "Son of God," given by the angel Gabriel when he announced the birth of Jesus to Mary, reveals the transcendent holiness of Jesus. But Gabriel also gave Jesus his name. "Jesus" means "God saves," and his name reveals Jesus' intimate relationship to the people he has come to unite to God.

These two aspects of Jesus—his holiness and his saving mission—are united in a very clear and moving way in the Book of Glory of the Gospel of John, chapters 13–20. Just as Moses passed on the divine legislation at the time of the manifestation of the divine holiness on Mount Sinai, Jesus gave his disciples his own commandments concerning holiness as his hour of glory on the cross began when he gave his disciples the Eucharist. When Jesus' disciples observe the commands of their holy master, they become not just servants, but friends. At the same time, they glorify the holiness of the Father himself.[18]

Jesus' Holiness Is the Source of Christian Ministry

The communication of Jesus' holiness, revealed by his life and teaching and reaching the culmination of revelation in his death on the cross, is carried out by the universal church. The church both preaches the word of God and celebrates the sacraments instituted by Christ. This is the way the Holy Spirit assures that Christ's pure doctrine is preserved in fulfillment of the words of Jesus to his disciples at the Last Supper:

> The Advocate, the Holy Spirit, whom the Father will send in my name, will teach you all things and remind you of all I have told you (Jn 14:26).

The Magisterium of the universal church has accurately and faithfully handed on Christ's teaching throughout all the generations (*CCC* 890-92). Furthermore, the liturgy of the church extends the risen Jesus' real, sacramental presence—the very touch of the living Jesus himself—to all who believe in his name.

In his Letter to the Romans, Paul described how God called people to become true images of his son Jesus. In so doing, he gave them grace to be holy so that eventually they would share the glory of Jesus himself (Rom 8: 28-30).

The on-going life of the church fulfills this teaching of Paul, and the total efficacy of the ministry of the Christian church and of all Christian ministers flows out of the holiness of Jesus. This is the meaning of the passage in John that describes an incident immediately after Jesus' crucifixion: When a soldier pierced the side of Jesus with a lance, blood and water flowed from it. This has been traditionally understood to signify the two great Christian sacraments: the Eucharist and baptism (Jn 19:34-36).

Paul compares the ministry of Moses and the Old Testament prophets with that of Jesus and his ministers. He sees Moses as administering a covenant of death. That is, unless one followed the Law exactly, fulfilling all its commands, the person would be doomed. Yet, the Law was given to Moses with the glory of the Lord impressed on the face of Moses by such a brightness that the Israelites could not bear looking at his face, though it was a brightness that faded. How much greater, then, will be the brightness that surrounds the administering of the Spirit which Jesus Christ gives to the world? And then Paul writes words that every minister of the gospel should ponder deeply in prayer. Speaking of all who believe in Jesus, Paul writes that we are turned into his image:

> We, with our unveiled faces reflecting like mirrors the brightness of the Lord, are being transformed from glory

to glory as we are turned into the image that we reflect (2 Cor 3:7-18).

Holiness Is Salvation—Salvation Is Holiness

To turn into the image of the Lord Jesus is to be saved. It is an on-going process of becoming holy as God is holy. Holiness is the mark of the children of God, and it is revealed in the kind of life we live, especially in loving our brothers and sisters. Without love, we cannot be holy as God is holy (1 Jn 3:7, 10-11).

Of course becoming holy as Jesus is holy is not something that can be done by our own power and under our own initiative, or even the power and initiative of the church and its ministers. This is a cardinal revelation of God, yet it is frequently disregarded in practice. The chapter on grace develops the proper understanding of God's saving work to make us holy as his new creation.

Here my point is that in order to be holy as God is holy, God must first reconcile us to himself. God must take the initiative just as he did with Abraham, because without the gift of his saving grace we are unholy. As Paul writes to the Corinthians, when we come to Christ, God creates anew. All our past sins are done away with, and we have a fresh start on a new life. This new life is a life of holiness that reflects the holiness of God himself. In fact, Paul puts it even more strongly: For our sake God made the sinless one into sin, so that in him we might become the holiness of God (2 Cor 5:17-21).

All of this is pretty heady teaching for the human mind. It takes faith to understand it, and it takes faith to accept it. God understands that, and so in his mercy he has given us the Holy Spirit which makes it possible for us to believe, understand and accept (1 Thes 4:7-8).

Furthermore, God has given us the church which passes on this revelation down through the centuries. The mystery of

Christ among us is a mystery—not because it is obscure, but because it is so rich in meaning for our lives that it had to be revealed slowly in a manner which makes it possible for us to appreciate the fullness of Christ and enter into union with him personally (Col 1:25-28).

Today in our parishes, God is relying on the parish team to communicate this message of holiness to all the people. It is a daunting challenge, but it is a challenge that can be happily met because of the power of the Holy Spirit at work in the people of God. As the team teaches this message of holiness, the team itself will grow in holiness and, therefore, in power to proclaim holiness more effectively.

The culmination of holiness, of course, will only be reached after our death and resurrection into the risen Jesus, and so Paul exhorts all the faithful:

> Let your thoughts be on things above, not on the things that are on the earth, because you have died, and now the life you have is hidden with Christ in God. But when Christ is revealed—and he is your life—you too will be revealed in glory with him (Col 3:2-4).

3

Grace Is Holiness Shared

Faith in Jesus Gives Joy to Life

*T*he purpose of communicating the divine holiness is to encourage believing Christians to have complete confidence in God's power to rescue us from our sins and make us holy, loving and happy.

One night, Nicodemus, impressed by the signs of power Jesus was working, came to Jesus to find out what they all meant. This was the occasion for Jesus to reveal the purpose of his coming on earth—to give eternal life to everyone who believes in him (Jn 3:16-18).

Too many sermons today say only one thing: "Try harder!" "Try harder" sermons are at the core of the decline of Christianity, being only endless challenges to do more. "Try harder" preaching does not proclaim the good news, it just passes out good advice. It does not proclaim the lordship of Jesus, only the responsibilities of humans. It is not concerned with revealing God's initiative in saving us from sin but with specifying our response to God's gifts. "Try harder" preaching does not focus on what God does for us, but emphasizes what we must do for God, and the avoidance of sin is given more importance than the experiencing of God's love.

Once I was trapped in the middle of a family fight that had evidently been raging for months. When the teenage daughter objected for the hundredth time to going to Mass on Sunday because she "didn't get anything out of it," her father, a staunch Catholic, finally yelled at her in exasperation: "Look, no one wants to go to Mass. You don't want to go to Mass. Your mother doesn't want to go Mass. I don't want to go to Mass. But as long as you are living under my roof and eating my food, you are going to Mass whether you like it or not, and I don't want to hear another word about it!"

Clearly, neither father nor daughter expected anything more out of going to Mass than the fulfillment of an unpleasant duty. The father was willing to endure going to Mass because he was sure he would be rewarded sometime in the future. The daughter was not, so she wanted out.

I discovered later that for both father and daughter all of religion was like the Mass, something tediously demanding. Fear made the father religious; boredom drove the daughter away. Neither heard Jesus say: "Come to me, all you who labor and are burdened, and I will give you rest" (Mt 11:28-30).

The truth of the matter is that believing in Jesus makes life easier to live, not harder. When we trust in Jesus, all things are transformed: suffering brings strength, poverty is enriching, terrors are laid to rest by love, and life gains meaning and purpose. In short, believers experience for themselves that Jesus does bestow a more abundant, full and rewarding life, as he promises: "I have come so that they may have life and have it to the full" (Jn 10:10).

Salvation is a totally free gift of God in both its beginnings and its ultimate effects. Our eternal happiness depends less on our weak wills and our uncertain constancy than on the unchanging foundation of God's unending love. Jesus says: "No one can come to me unless he is drawn by the Father who sent me, and I will raise him up on the last day" (Jn 6:44).

Christian Life Is a Gift of God[1]

Our lives as Christians in this world are the fruit of God's love. Each day, we who believe in Jesus are transformed by his love so that in God's time and in God's way we become the images of his Son Jesus, which he has willed us to be from all eternity. Since his love in our hearts is the sure sign of God's presence, and since the other gifts of the Spirit are the effects of his saving activity within us, we who believe can rest secure in the knowledge that through faith in Jesus Christ, we are being delivered from sin and prepared for an eternal life of happiness. St. Paul assures us that because God did not spare his own Son, but gave him up to benefit us all, we may be certain that he will not refuse us anything. Not only did Christ die for us, however, he also rose from the dead, and now he stands at the right hand of God the Father and makes constant intercession for us, pleading with the Father for everything that we need to become holy. Therefore, even if we are troubled or worried, or being persecuted, or lacking food or clothes, or being threatened or even attacked, Jesus is still with us; these things are only passing trials which we will be able to overcome because of the power of Jesus who loves us so much. At the conclusion of this teaching, Paul is so overwhelmed by the greatness of God's gift that he bursts out in a canticle of praise:

> For I am certain of this: neither death nor life, no angel, no prince, nothing that exists, nothing still to come, not any power, or height or depth, nor any created thing can ever come between us and the love of God made visible in Christ Jesus our Lord (Rom 8:31-39).

No wonder each one of us can say with genuine joy: "Thank God! He loves me!"

God Is All-Knowing and All-Powerful[2]

Scripture tells us that because God is an intelligent being, he has a plan. The all-powerful Creator of the entire world and everything in it has created a master design to reflect his glory and his power and his love. However, we human beings have trouble grasping God's plan because it is so far beyond our wildest dreams or imaginings. We live in a world which God created "very good"[3] but which human sin has terribly distorted. Every day we see countless manifestations of weakness and sometimes malice: war, ethnic cleansing, racial prejudice, exploitation, sensuality, stupidity and alienation. Consequently, it is difficult for us to see beyond human failure and even faintly conceive of the absolute power, wisdom and goodness of God.

Yet, this absolute goodness is the basis for all that happens in the world and to us, and unless we appreciate the greatness of the One by whom we have been created, we can never fully appreciate the greatness of the love that gave us life. Nothing can escape the notice or power of God. He is all, and not even human freedom can possibly frustrate or change God's overarching will.[4]

Human Beings Are Truly Free

At the same time, both our experience of life and the revelation of sacred scripture make it clear that we are truly free. In fact, our very freedom is the cause of much anguish as we try to figure out what we should do. Career choices, for example, are not limited to young people deciding on the future. Even adults have to make serious choices about jobs and families, and sometimes those choices are very difficult. Devout Christians, trusting in God's guidance, try to make those choices as a discernment of God's will for themselves and those they love. Such choices, then, are made in the light of eternity and eternal life.[5]

Jesus Reconciles Human Freedom and God's Infallible Will[6]

These two seemingly opposite, contradictory truths— that we have free will, but that God's will prevails wherever we do good—lie at the heart of understanding the ways of God with us.[7] They must be reconciled, brought together into a single vision of reality, a perspective which permits us to see and to experience the dignity and wonder of the Creator/Father and his creatures/children—men and women, you and me.

That fusion of divine power and human freedom is brought about in Jesus Christ through love. God is love. He created a world of beauty and order to share his own fullness of life—his own being—with those he has called into existence. The apex of this creative design of love is a human—Jesus Christ. To the Christians at Ephesus, a writer inspired by God himself summarizes in moving language and vivid images the greatness and scope of the divine plan of salvation.[8]

God had always intended to share his glory with his human creatures; his deepest desire was that we would be his adopted children and live through love in his presence. He wanted us to be as holy as he is holy. To that end, the Father sent his Beloved Son, Jesus Christ, to die on a cross, to rid the world of evil and division and give all human beings the chance to enter into the freedom of eternal life. Again and again, in this passage, the writer emphasizes that God did not have to do any of this, but because of his infinite love, he chose us. Furthermore, as a testimony to that divine and free choice, God sent the Holy Spirit to dwell in our hearts and make us conscious that our life will not end with death, but will go beyond the grave where we will live forever with God. This is salvation, and for this salvation we give praise to our Father.

It is in Christ Jesus that human freedom and divine power are brought together, for Jesus is both God and man. In him, through faith, we achieve the perfection of our humanity which is in fact a sharing in the perfection of God. Because Jesus is the image of God, if we want to know what God looks like, how God acts, what God expects of us, we have only to look to Jesus.[9] And Jesus is not hard to find. We find him in the scriptures, of course, and we find Jesus in the church, particularly in the liturgy. Christ is present in the Sacrifice of the Mass. By his power he is present in the sacraments so that when anybody baptizes it is really Christ himself who baptizes. He is present in his word since it is Jesus himself who speaks when the holy scriptures are read in the church. Lastly, Jesus is present when the church prays and sings. "Where two or three are gathered together in my name, there I am in the midst of them" (Mt 18:20).

God's Love Guides Our Lives

Whereas the perfection of God is absolute love and total knowledge, human perfection is very limited. God sees all reality in one constant vision like a beautiful and completed tapestry hanging on a wall; we perceive only the laborious process of weaving the one small strand of our lives, day by day, while missing the great total effect. As a result, we find our strength flagging and our resolve weakening. We are free to weave our strand here or there only because we do not perceive the whole effort. Yet, the master weaver does see all, and his love gently guides our free designs so that we create the perfect vision he has conceived from all eternity, each creature contributing inexorably to the whole.[10]

God Chooses To Share His Holiness Freely

Yet, because of his love, God is not content with the simple, blind carrying out of his plan.[11] God's will is a wise and loving plan to which, in the final analysis, all creatures contribute. God has freely chosen to bring believers to the absolute height of the experience of love by revealing to them the design of his tapestry, the hidden plan of his purpose, the inner workings of the divine mind through Jesus Christ.

This revelation of the divine plan is the work of the parish team. Just as Paul in times past revealed the mystery to those communities he served,[12] so also ministers of the word today reveal the mystery to the communities they serve. In this key ministry of faith, members of the parish team find the source of their own dignity and the importance of their work on behalf of the gospel.

Scripture calls this special election "God's mercy" (1 Pet 2:10) in order to emphasize that it is something to which we do not have an innate right. We are not dealing with human equity, but divine holiness, divine majesty, divine generosity. In the long history of God's dealings with men and women, his choice, to whatever purpose, is frequently not in accord with human expectations or desires, and certainly not the result of merit. Indeed, those who have been designated for a special task may not even be aware of God's designs. To believers, however, a rich passage from Paul's Letter to the Romans reveals the full import of God's freedom in assigning to his creatures their places in the working out of his loving plan for all. For example, before either Jacob or Esau was born, God told Rebecca that her younger son, Jacob, would be served by his elder brother. This was a clear violation of the prevailing custom, whereby the oldest child was the primary inheritor of property and leadership. Scripture says that God did this so that it would be clear to all that he is sovereignly free to do anything he wants. God is not subject to human rules, regulations, customs or expectations.

And God cannot be considered unjust in doing this because everything he does for us is the result of his loving mercy and is always for our good without regard to whether or not we are worthy. Paul sums it up when he writes, "The only thing that counts is not what human beings want or try to do, but the mercy of God" (Rom 9:10-18).

Now this teaching of scripture is difficult to understand. We might immediately jump to the conclusion: So what I do makes no difference at all! But that would not be true, as we shall see.

Sin Holds Us Trapped in Our Failures

The mercy that God shows to his chosen ones is healing. Probably anyone who reads this book has an intense desire to do good, live a holy life, be pleasing to God and thereby achieve eternal happiness. Yet, when we are perfectly honest, how many of us are holy enough to be confident that God will reward us? Many lives—even outwardly good lives—are built on a fear that we really are not doing enough to please God, that we have not quite come up to his expectations for us. We do try to be good, but we also are aware of our weakness and constant failures. I lose my temper when I least expect to. I find I cannot really give the help to someone in my family that I should. I am selfish when I would rather be generous. I have a habit of sin I cannot break. In short, I have turned out to be a disappointment to myself, my family and God.

If, therefore, eternal happiness is going to depend on my response to what God has given me—the use of my talents, my avoidance of sin—then my fears are well-grounded because my weak will is not really up to being perfect as my heavenly Father is perfect, and the effort to be perfect in the face of repeated failure produces profound spiritual anxiety and depression.

Now, obviously, we cannot heal ourselves. Our limitations are not something we can cast off because we want to. A one-legged man cannot decide to grow another leg, a blind man cannot decide to see, a sinner cannot force himself to be a saint. Some things are beyond our power, which is why we find ourselves enslaved by failure and inadequacy. Biblically speaking, this limiting power that prevents the full exercise of our goodness, and, therefore, the achievement of happiness, is called sin.

So powerful is the influence of sin in our lives that Paul describes it as a slave master. It makes us do things we hate to do, yet we still do them. If you have ever tried to give up smoking, you know what Paul means. It took me five efforts over a period of ten years just to stop smoking—and sin is harder to stop than smoking! And it is precisely because of the power of sin in our lives that God sent Jesus Christ to be our savior (cf. Rom 7: 14-24).

Jesus Heals and Gives New Life

Jesus Christ is the healer, the rescuer. He lifts us up out of the morass of failure and sin by transforming our attitudes and redirecting our desires by his power. Consequently, we no longer live for this life alone, which leads to death, but in him we direct our energies to a heavenly goal, which is eternal life (*CCC* 654).

When we believe in Jesus, he opens the eyes of our mind and we see all reality in a new light—the light that reveals the purpose of life (cf. 2 Cor 4:6). By trusting in him, we are given new power to act—his power. Faith is trust, an experience that Jesus is acting in me according to his promise so that I literally live his life and love with his love.

This trust in God's love is particularly important when we are discouraged by the pain of life or are actually suffering, either mentally or physically. So important is the role of suffering in the development of Christian spirituality that Paul actually boasts of his own sufferings because his sufferings—like our own—bring us closer to Jesus through the Holy Spirit. He writes: "Sufferings bring patience, as we know, and patience brings perseverance, and perseverance brings hope, and this hope is not deceptive, because the love of God has been poured into our hearts by the Holy Spirit which has been given to us" (Rom 5:1-11). The Holy Spirit gives us such joy and peace that we know we have been reconciled to God through faith in Jesus Christ.

Moreover, in talking to his disciples, Jesus did not limit the trust they put in him to just the unseen spiritual realities—things that were difficult to verify by the hard experience of real life. He wanted them to trust in him for all things as a sign of that inner trust in his ultimate healing. He told them not to worry about getting food or clothing. He promised his disciples that because his Father knows we need these things, if we set out hearts on the kingdom, God will provide everything we need. Therefore, "Fear not, little flock" (Lk 12:22-32).

Our Works Are the Fruit of Christ's Life[13]

Having given us the kingdom, God also gives us the power to win it. This is perhaps the key to the relationship of good works and faith. When a person is healed of blindness, that person can now do things he or she could never do before. The newly sighted can go where they want without being led by the hand; they can undertake new works, evaluate and judge things hidden from them before. Literally, the newly sighted are new persons: no longer dependent on others, but independent, able to walk without stumbling because they have the light. So, too, when we put on the mind of Christ and live by Christ's light, we acquire new values and judge things in a different way.

Suffering Unites Us to God

After his conversion to Christ, St. Paul saw suffering not as an evil, but as a way to union with God (*CCC* 1508, 1521). Consequently, he embraced pain, hardship and loss with joy and thanksgiving. He wrote to the Philippians: "All I want is to know Christ and the power of his resurrection and to share his sufferings by reproducing the pattern of his death. That is the way I can hope to take my place in the resurrection of the dead" (Phil 3:8-12).

How different is Paul's attitude of willing surrender from the stoic endurance of pain and the desperate search for relief that characterizes a world stumbling about in the darkness of fear and unbelief. And it is this attitude of willing surrender that the parish team should encourage in all those who suffer. Some suffering simply cannot be removed; it is a painful situation that can only be adjusted to. So the parish team by its teaching and preaching should give all sufferers the consolation of Paul's teaching on suffering as a way to deeper union with Christ in both his death and his resurrection. For truly, when we die to ourselves for Christ's sake, we really do experience, even in our pain, something of the joy of the resurrection.

The Light of Christ Gives Life

This light of Christ, however, is not a once-given light. It is a continuing radiation of divine light, leading us every step of the way, all the time, so that at no point can we say, "I'll take over now and do it on my own." That would be to revert to darkness. But healed by the light, and filled with light, I can do what I never could do when I was in the darkness. In other words, by filling me with light, Jesus also fills me with the works of the light and enables me to do those works of light because I see with his eyes and his mind and live his love.

So great is the change that God brings about in us that scripture refers to it as a new creation, a birth into a new life. It is life in the Spirit which will never end, and it is a totally free gift—a complete favor, an undeserved and unmerited grace. The Letter to the Ephesians stresses this when it says:

> It is by grace that you have been saved, through faith; not by anything of your own, but by a gift from God; not by anything that you have done, so that nobody can claim the credit. We are God's work of art, created in Christ Jesus to live the good life as from the beginning he had meant us to live it (Eph 2:8-10).

God Moves Us Freely To Fulfill His Infallible Plan

What a mystery! God has made us free, and in accord with the free nature that he has given us, he moves us infallibly to accomplish what he has willed from all eternity. "It is God, for his own loving purpose, who puts both the will and the action into you" (Phil 2:13). Because we are free, he moves us gently but relentlessly to our appointed ends—freely but surely! And so powerful is this movement of grace that we become a new creation: our sins are forgiven and we live with the life of Christ himself in us (2 Cor 5:17-21).

To become the goodness of God—this is why we were chosen! This is why the gift of the Spirit has been given to us! This is why we have the power to love: to be like God, to be holy as God is Holy!

If our salvation and perseverance in good works depended on the strength of our weak and vacillating will, we would indeed have good cause to fear the last judgment. If it were up to the quality of my love, I would be dubious about the outcome. If salvation were predicated on my response to his words, then I am certainly to be pitied, for I have failed again and again by broken promises and forgotten resolutions.

But it is not my weak human and faltering love that makes the difference. It is God's strong, endless and everlasting love poured forth into my soul by the Holy Spirit when I believe in Jesus that makes the difference. My love for my neighbor is the effect of God's love in me—the sign of his presence and the guarantee of his care and power in my life. The First Letter of John says: "God is love, and anyone who lives in love lives in God, and God lives in him" (1 Jn 4:15-21). Chosen and transformed, my very desires directed toward heaven with confidence even in the midst of suffering, I can look forward to happiness here and hereafter because already I share God's glory through my gift of faith.

With this understanding of God's saving initiative in our life, his shaping us through love to be the perfect images of his Son Jesus, there is always the possibility of self-deception. Because it is mystery, and we are basically simple folk who like to make things as easy as possible for ourselves, there is always the chance that we will simply lie back and say, "Save me," without appreciating that salvation consists in the happiness that comes from the life of faith-filled virtue and the exercise of the gifts of the Spirit. In other words, in giving us the eternal gift of salvation, God gives us the energy and the desire to perform those works of virtue that bring peace and happiness to us and to others. For only the holy person can be the truly happy person—here or hereafter.

The Spirit Gives Us Signs That He Is at Work in Us[14]

Consequently, St. Paul in his Letter to the Galatians gives us certain signs by which we can always test to see if we are in fact walking in accord with the wisdom of God which leads to life, and not simply following the impulses of our own weak will which end in death. If we give in to the movements of our fleshly desires, we will not be able to enter the kingdom of God. Such things as fornication, impurity, licentiousness, idolatry, sorcery, enmity, strife, jealousy, anger, selfishness, dissension, envy, drunkenness, carousing, and the like lead to death of the spirit.

On the other hand, if we live by the Spirit of God, we will enjoy the fruits of the Spirit: love, joy, peace, patience, kindness, goodness, faithfulness, gentleness, self-control. Consequently, it is an essential part of Christian asceticism to "crucify" or refuse to give in to passions and desires that work against the Spirit of Christ in us.[15] And those who belong to Christ Jesus have crucified the flesh with its passions and desires.

God Moves Us Both To Desire and To Act

How deep is the mystery of predestination we have explored! How convenient it would be to say that we simply merited heaven by our works, or to say that God gives it to us all without any effort on our part. Yet, the truth of the mystery unites the two: God moves us to desire, to act and to achieve in a way which intimately involves our own efforts, as we have already seen in the text from his Letter to the Philippians:

> Work for your salvation in fear and trembling. It is God, for his own loving purpose, who puts both the will and the action into you (Phil 2:12-13).

Because we do have our share in the work of salvation, always under God's movement, it is appropriate for Christians to pray for one another. We pray that God will give us the strength and the courage to follow the gospel no matter what the circumstances that discourage us. The life of virtue is not for the faint-hearted; even our perseverance in virtue is the fruit of God's grace at work in our hearts, minds and lives (Col 1:9-14).

We Cannot Fully Understand the Mystery of Predestination

But the question is, "Why?" Why does God's grace seem to bear fruit in some and not in others? Granted that God is free to do what he wills and no human being can oppose him, why does he treat different persons in different ways? Why are some people beautiful, rich and generous, and others poor, sickly and selfish?

There is, of course, no clear and easy answer. Paul, after considering the questions deeply in his Letter to the Romans, seems finally to throw up his hands in praise at ever fathoming the divine mind when he says:

> How rich are the depths of God! How deep are his wisdom and knowledge, and how impossible to penetrate his motives or understand his methods! Who could ever know the mind of the Lord? Who could ever be his counselor? Who could ever give him anything or lend him anything? All that exists comes from him; all is by him and for him. To him be glory for ever! Amen (Rom 11:33-36).

Indeed, we humans have always asked the question: "Why?" When Job thought he was being rejected by God, all his friends gathered around him and told him he must have sinned. In fact, even Jesus' own disciples thought all suffering was caused by sin. When they saw a man who had been blind from birth, they asked, "Rabbi, who sinned, this man or his parents, for him to have been born blind?" Jesus answered, "Neither he nor his parents sinned; he was born

blind so that the works of God might be displayed in him"
(Jn 9:2-3).

Jesus always answered in the same vein. Although God is
sovereignly free to bestow his gifts wherever he wills, his gifts
always reveal his glory, power and love. Since the greatest of
God's gifts is Jesus Christ, it follows that all who believe in
Jesus experience the full glory of God himself—imperfectly in
this life, perfectly in the next.[16]

There Are Limits to Our Testing of God

Paul, on the other hand, is quite blunt about the limits
we creatures have in questioning God about his intentions.
We are like clay in the potter's hand, and just as the clay cannot demand that it be made into a certain shape, neither can
we as creatures of God. Yet we are not clay and God is not a
potter. Although God is all-powerful and could easily destroy
anyone who attempted to thwart the perfection of the divine
plan, he does not. He deals with us with infinite patience,
showing his mercy to all those whom he has called to be his
people (cf. Rom 9:20-24).

Whatever the abstract, theological problems that are
raised by the concept of predestination,[17] the holy Bible always
addresses itself to the question of what God is doing personally for me and what I am doing for others. The life and death
of each of us has its influence on others; at the same time we
belong to the Lord. So Christ both died and came to life. By
his death and resurrection, God made Jesus Lord of both the
dead and the living (cf. Rom 14:7-9).

The question, therefore, is not impersonal speculation
about divine justice or injustice, universal salvation, or the
case of the aboriginal savage in a far-off land who has never
had the opportunity to hear the gospel message. The real
question is what I, a believer, have done and am doing with

my precious gifts of the Spirit given in baptism to aid my neighbor to come to a knowledge of the truth that will make him free (cf. Jn 8:32). What have I done to share my experience of faith in Jesus Christ with over one hundred million fellow-Americans who have not accepted Jesus Christ as their Lord and Savior?

Obviously, then, this is precisely the question the parish team needs to address. The preaching of the team is God's chosen instrument for bringing salvation to those who have not yet come to Jesus, for whatever reason. It is a great responsibility, but it is also a great joy because the preaching occurs under the movement of the Holy Spirit who wishes that the whole world might be saved—through faith (cf. Jn 3:16-18).

God Wants To Bring Salvation to All[18]

Revelation assures us that no matter how mysterious it seems to our limited minds, God's plan is to bring happiness to all. St. Paul tells Timothy: "He wants everyone to be saved and reach full knowledge of the truth" (1 Tim 2:4). Yet his gift of salvation is being offered to evil and contrary people at war with each other and with God. Consequently, the manner of bestowing the gift quite transcends our understanding. However, this gift of salvation begins with the experience itself that God is indeed Love and that his love is always exercised for our good.[19]

Reading the Bible Helps Growth in Holiness

No one book can possibly summarize the teaching of the sacred scriptures and the church or hope to answer all the questions raised by the mystery we have been considering. Touching as we have the most secret intentions of the inexhaustible divine mind and the most profound depths of infinite divine love, we can only trust that as we grow in the Lord, all will be revealed to us in the Spirit. For this reason, in addition to the usual sacramental life of Catholics, the church urges each of us to read the sacred scriptures each day. From the scriptures we learn God's own wisdom that leads to salvation through faith in Christ Jesus. Furthermore, we are not drawing our wisdom from literature conceived by the human mind alone. All scripture is inspired by God; therefore, it is the richest possible source for guiding people's lives and teaching them to be holy. If a person would want the best possible preparation for ministry, Paul in his second letter to Timothy says that the best preparation is to know sacred scripture (cf. 2 Tim 3:15-17).

The parish team, therefore, should vigorously promote both the personal reading of the Bible and small-group Bible sharing. Both activities have the additional blessing of disposing the parishioners to be attentive to the word of God in the liturgical acts of the parish. Whether the Bible sharing is directly biblically based or done through the lectionary, greater familiarity with the words of scripture should be a parish priority.

As we search the scriptures in order to enter more fully into the mystery of Christ saving us and making us holy, St. Paul's prayer for his beloved Ephesians remains a prayer for each of us:

> According to the wealth of his glory, may he give you the power through his Spirit for your inner person to grow strong, so that Christ may make his home in your hearts through faith, and then, rooted in love and founded on love, may you together with all the saints have strength to grasp the breadth and the length, the height and the depth, and to know the surpassing knowledge of Christ's love so you may be filled with the fullness of God.
>
> Glory be to him whose power, working in us, can do far more than we can ask or conceive; glory be to him in the church and in Christ Jesus through all generations for ever and ever. Amen (Eph 3:16-21).

4

Reconciliation Leads to Holiness

*T*he parish team can bring some really great news to the parish when it communicates the good news of reconciliation. Sin is a tremendous problem in the contemporary world, as violent crimes, scandals and domestic crises attest. But the good news is that no matter how evil things are, Jesus Christ died to save sinners, and no sinner need ever fear rejection. When Jesus was accused of encouraging sin because he ate and drank—we would say today, "partied"—with sinners, Jesus told the powerful parable of his love for sinners and his desire for their reconciliation with God. Just as a shepherd leaves a hundred sheep to search for one lost sheep until he finds it, so God also seeks out the lost sinners. "There will be more joy in heaven over one sinner who repents than over ninety-nine righteous people who have no need to repent" (Lk: 15:4-7).

As members of the church, the parish formation team is a powerful minister of reconciliation.[1] Not only do the team members together preach reconciliation through the words of scripture and the teaching of the church, perhaps even more effectively they witness to the power of Jesus' reconciliation by the joyful witness of their own lives as repentant sinners. Having experienced forgiveness themselves, they can speak with authority and yet with compassion about sin. To discuss sin today from a Christian perspective is very difficult,[2] given some serious misunderstandings about sin and its harmful effects on both the sinner and others that are touched by the sinner's wrongdoing. The church—like Jesus himself—must condemn sin in all its forms; at the same time, it must ever extend the merciful hand of God, always granting forgiveness to sinners who repent.

Indeed the first preaching of Jesus recorded in the Gospel of Mark is, "This is the time of fulfillment. The reign of God is at hand! Reform your lives and believe in the gospel" (Mk 1:15).

Since we live in the time of fulfillment, we are called by Jesus to continually reform our lives and increase our faith in him. It is in this context of the saving power of God that the parish team forms the parish to hunger for and expect the mercy of God.

Sin and its harmful and damaging effects cannot be ignored in parish preaching, although it sometimes is because of a fear of offending. Too many people suffer from the effects of sin—both their own sins and the sins of others. So sin is very serious business. At the same time, forgiveness of sin is equally serious business, and forgiveness is why people come to Jesus Christ. People come to the church and its sacrament of reconciliation because they hunger for forgiveness and they yearn for deliverance from the power of sin in their lives.

The parish team, therefore, offers one of its most valuable services when it gives to those it serves a balanced view of sin and salvation. It needs to avoid both harsh condemnation of the sinner and a sentimentalizing of the evil of sin. Always it has to hold out Jesus' own promise of forgiveness to the repentant as well as a timely warning to the unrepentant of the consequences of sin. This is a grave responsibility, similar to that given to the prophet Ezekiel. God appointed him to be a watchman for Israel and to give the people warning. He was to warn the wicked that they would die if they persisted in their sin; if he did not warn the sinner, the wicked person would die for the sin, but the prophet himself would be held responsible for the death.[3] It was not an easy task, and Ezekiel suffered in responding to God's charge. Nor is it an easy and comfortable task today. Nevertheless, it is an essential part of communicating God's grace to make people holy temples of God in a world in which sin is not a rare experience.

The Origin of Sin

The *locus classicus* for the Christian understanding of sin is found in the ancient myth[4] concerning the fall of the first man and woman: Adam, Eve and the forbidden fruit.[5]

The story itself is so well-known that it does not require repeating here. What is important about the story, however, is how the psychological dynamics portrayed in that ancient myth (which, nevertheless, is divinely revealed truth) are repeated again and again in human history. It is a divine story revealing the inner workings of the sinful heart.

First, of course, there is the temptation: to eat the luscious fruit (to drink, to engage in irresponsible sexual behavior, to embezzle). The temptation always allures with promises of greater happiness, in spite of the fact that the contemplated action has been forbidden by God.

Next, there is the examination of the illicit offer (always recognized somehow as forbidden, illicit, shady or questionable), and then the sinner's assent to specific actions, followed by eating the fruit (buying the gun, stealing the car, going up to the apartment).

Frequently, someone else is included in the plans to assist in the execution of the plot: Adam eats too (the sex partner says yes, the confederate drives the getaway car, the accountant agrees to juggle the books).

Often, the after-effects are not as fulfilling as the promise: the fruit did not confer godhood (the partner had herpes, the confederate wants a bigger cut, the client suspects fraud).

Then come the excuses: the woman made me eat it, the serpent made me do it (we're in love, I needed the money, everybody's doing it).

But the end result is the same whether one is caught or not, whether the offense is great or small: a new element of selfishness, distrust and coarseness enters into all the human relationships of the sinner. The sinner is less human than before the fall; he or she is to some extent the victim of the sin. And the power of evil grows over the face of the earth.

Adam and Eve were excluded from the fullness of life they formerly knew: the innocence of nudity is no longer theirs and life is extremely difficult. The very things that are most necessary for survival—working the land for food, bearing children—become the most burdensome. Human joy is henceforth tinged with sorrow and pain.

And the instances of evil multiplied, as is so often the case whenever sin is committed. First, their son Cain killed his brother Abel, and after that general corruption covered the earth until the Lord God had to cover the earth with water to stop the flood of evil.

The Effects of the Fall Never Cease

The consequences of this first fall continue until today; they form a major focus of scripture and Christian theological development.[6] Christian revelation acknowledges the curse of Genesis: childbirth is painful for women; women and men have to work for a living; they are attractive to one another, but struggle with issues of power and control in their relationships. And over all of us lies the inevitable end of our life—we will die (cf. Gen 3:16-19).

At the same time, as St. Paul writes to the Romans, we yearn to be free. We want to be able to enjoy all the good things of creation and to look forward confidently to the end of suffering and to share eternal glory with God our Father (Rom 8:20–21).

To some, it may seem incredible that an offense committed so long ago should have such cosmic consequences. Yet no sin is without serious ramifications for the innocent as well as for the guilty. How many little offenses suddenly are discovered to have coalesced into a way of life. An almost idle adulterous encounter suddenly breeds incredible complications. Indeed, such complications are integral to many of the plots of more than one television soap opera. Financial empires have collapsed because they were built on a few acts of insider-trading.

There was a banker who committed fraud and was caught and sentenced to jail. Since he had been a very respected member of the community, it was a tremendous loss of prestige to himself, but an even greater source of shame to his wife and children. They were ridiculed by their peers to such an extent that the mother and children had to leave the community that the banker-father-husband had defrauded.

While the move brought them relief from community pressure, never again was the family able to achieve the level of income, power or respect that it had once enjoyed. Because the son's education had been so badly disrupted, he never went on to college. When his children were born, they, too, never had the opportunity to live at the level of prosperity and respect the banker had originally attained. Although the grandchildren were not personally responsible, they certainly suffered the consequences of their grandfather's sin and were bitter because of it.

As the evil stemming from the "original sin" spread over the earth, its effects multiplied. The lust, greed and fear that were released by that first act of rebellion against God produced dictatorships, spawned nationalistic dreams of conquest, generated wars, wasted natural resources, and polluted the environment.

Events and attitudes throughout history have shaped us to be the people we are today. We are the inheritors of civilizations that were built, in part, on sinful attitudes. As a result, our values are as corrupt as the civilizations which produced them, and we add our own corruptions.

A Ray of Hope in Eden

Even in the darkest hour of the fall when Adam and Eve were driven from the garden of Eden, the merciful and compassionate God gave them hope of salvation: the famous *protevangelium:*

> Then the Lord God said to the serpent, " I shall put enmity between you and the woman, and between your offspring and hers; he will strike at your head, and you will strike his heel" (Gen 3:15).

In this brief passage, the church fathers see the promise of redemption in Jesus Christ. Jesus is the offspring of Eve, and Jesus will ultimately attack the serpent's offspring—the powers of evil in our own day—and destroy them. And the instrument of destruction for the powers of evil was Jesus' own death on the cross.[7]

Unresolved Guilt Prolongs the Pain of Sin

Today many people are suffering terribly from the pain of unresolved guilt that expresses itself in many diverse ways and in varying degrees of intensity. Sometimes guilt is experienced only as a vague, nagging anxiety about life; there is an uncomfortable awareness that something is wrong, but no clear idea of what is wrong. At other times, it leads to fears about the future because one feels inadequate to deal with the problems that may come up. Depression is another symptom that something is wrong; some of that is due to physical causes, but others suffer depression from a feeling of guilt that has never been honestly faced and dealt with. Today thousands of suffering Americans are receiving some kind of psychiatric or psychological treatment. For many, counseling has been going on for years without any change in the fundamental condition.

Sometimes the feelings of guilt are inappropriate because the person is truly not responsible for his or her actions, even if they harm others. Obsessive-compulsive behavior, for example, is a reality that finds its origins in a complex of genetic and environmental factors, and such uncontrolled conduct has extensive ramifications in terms of the obsessive person's relations with his or her fellow human beings: family, friends, co-workers and even perfect strangers. There is well-validated clinical evidence that many evil actions flow from factors over which an individual really has no control.

To Be Human Is To Be Responsible

This is true of many, but certainly not all evil actions. At least some actions of all but completely demented persons are under the control of the individual and result from personal free decisions. These free decisions can be sinful to a greater or lesser degree, and in these cases a sense of guilt is clearly appropriate.

Catholic moral theology has always recognized that "a lack of full awareness and deliberate consent" lessens human responsibility in particular acts (*CCC* 1735). As Pope John Paul II teaches:

Clearly, situations can occur which are very complex and obscure from a psychological viewpoint, and which influence the sinner's subjective imputability.[8]

Since parish team members reveal the holiness of God in the context of American culture, to be effective it is vital that members of the parish formation team take into account how their listeners have been shaped, probably unconsciously, by social attitudes with regard to personal responsibility for one's actions.[9] Human holiness depends on one's response to divine holiness; sin is the lack of that response or a positive rejection. So, if listeners are not convinced that they are responsible for their actions and can control their behavior, they will not be able to respond to the saving grace of Jesus Christ who died to save sinners from their sins.

Pope John Paul II puts it this way:

It not possible to deal with sin and conversion only in abstract terms. In the concrete circumstances of sinful humanity in which there can be no conversion without the acknowledgment of one's own sin, The church's ministry of reconciliation intervenes in each individual case with a precise penitential purpose...to the rejection of evil, to the reestablishment of friendship with God, to a new interior ordering, to a fresh ecclesial conversion. Indeed, even beyond the boundaries of the church and the community of believers, the message and ministry of penance are addressed to all men and women, because all need conversion and reconciliation.[10]

American Culture Fosters Loss of Personal Responsibility

The true evil of sin is not appreciated today because so often the popular mind has become accustomed to calling the grossest sinful behavior with the most far-reaching results only a "mistake." Frequently it characterizes a sinful act as an "error of judgment" or a "misunderstanding." It reduces vices, such as drug abuse and sexual molestation, that constitute ways of life to "problems" or "illnesses."

Sometimes an individual's personal responsibility for harmful action is explained away as the result of environmental factors which make the perpetrator of crime as much a victim as the one he or she has victimized.

At the same time, contemporary society abets the sinner's denial by proposing complex justifications which lessen and eventually deny personal responsibility. Historian Paul Johnson attributes this historically sudden lessening of personal responsibility to two major movements at the beginning of the twentieth century. Karl Marx replaced personal responsibility with the inevitability of class conflict. Of greater importance to western civilization, Sigmund Freud replaced it with psychological forces. Johnson writes:

> In the Freudian analysis, the personal conscience, which stood at the very heart of the Judeo-Christian ethic and was the principal engine of individualistic achievement, was dismissed as a mere safety-device, collectively created, to protect civilized order from the fearful aggressiveness of human beings....It might be, as sociologists were already suggesting, that society could be collectively guilty in creating conditions which made crime and vice inevitable. But personal guilt-feelings were an illusion to be dispelled. None of us were individually guilty; we were all guilty.[11]

There is certainly no doubt that progress in the scientific understanding of human psychology has enabled us to identify, treat and, to a greater or lesser extent, modify a wide variety of deviant human behavior patterns.[12]

Psychiatry and psychology have made important contributions to the diagnosis of mental illness and have made vast strides in developing therapeutic techniques aimed at behavior modification without assigning blame for irresponsible actions. Yet, how much have they actually helped? Bellah reports mixed results:

> The increase in psychological sophistication has apparently brought an increase in feelings of personal well-being. But there is a cost. Anxiety and uncertainty about more important and enduring relationships are increasing rather than decreasing.[13]

In a footnote, Bellah observes:

> Americans experience more doubt about who they "really" are and more difficulty in finding an authentic self. Thus over time guilt declines but anxiety increases.[14]

Karl Menninger, M.D., a professional psychiatrist and founder of the world-famous Menninger Clinic, perhaps best expresses a learned contemporary understanding of one of the basic operative components of what Christians have traditionally identified as sin which violates God's holiness:

> The willful disregard or sacrifice of the welfare of others for the welfare or satisfaction of the self is an essential quality of the concept *sin*.[15]

Lack of Responsibility Has Serious Consequences

This understanding is exemplified in the case of a man who had gotten into the habit of drinking a great deal in college as part of the campus social life. When he went to work for a large company, alcohol continued to be an important part of his social milieu. Over the years, this resulted in a true addiction to alcohol. When he got married and began to have children, the pressures of family and competition at his place of business combined to increase his need for alcohol and his dependence on it.

As his drunken behavior became more frequent and more bizarre, he caused tremendous strains in his relationships with his wife and children and business associates. Although he was aware of his addiction, he did nothing to lessen his dependency, particularly since drinking was an accepted part of his social and business environment.

Eventually, however, the stress in the family became too great to endure, and his wife divorced him, taking the children, who had been badly damaged both psychologically and physically by his drunken outbursts. One night, after he had destroyed his family and was seeking solace once again in alcohol, the man drove while extremely drunk into a school bus that was returning from an outing. He killed a large number of children.

Since he was drunk as a result of the disease of alcoholism, the question was asked: How responsible was he for his harmful behavior?

Was It Sin?

The Christian response to whether this was a sin is: Yes, since he never wanted effectively to change his behavior pattern by giving up alcohol. The legal response was punishment for criminal behavior resulting in deaths. The victims' families' response was a call for his death.

This graphic and somewhat fictionalized example, of course, could be repeated regarding other harmful and criminal behavior. Other elements lessening responsibility can be put forward to excuse perpetrators of business fraud, the so-called "victimless" white-collar crimes of financial manipulation, tax evasion, sexual promiscuity—indeed, the entire range of human action. Yet, the fact remains that the criminal does inflict harm on other individuals, on society and on himself or herself.

Whatever factors may lessen responsibility for human action, all of which have been carefully delineated in Christian moral tradition,[16] human beings remain accountable for what they do in courts of law, social convention and religion.

Sin Separates the Sinner from the Holiness of God

As we have seen in the earlier chapters, the goal of all human life is to be holy as God is holy. The goal is to have the joy, peace and love that is proper to God himself by sharing in God's own holiness. The parish team members have the opportunity to be instruments of God's holiness and, therefore, to share in the joy, peace and love of the ministry of formation. The task is not done alone and unaided. Always the team is empowered by the grace of the Holy Spirit, and the Spirit brings about the fruitful effects of the team's work on behalf of the gospel. The only thing that blocks growth in holiness and its fruits is sin. Christian tradition, unfolding in all ages the basic biblical teaching, defines sin in terms of opposition to the holiness of God. Sin is unholiness; it separates the sinner from the divine. "Perverse thoughts separate us from God" (Wis 1:3).

Furthermore, only when Christians comprehend the radical malice of sin can they cherish the saving work of Jesus Christ who died precisely to save us from our sins. "Through his blood, we gain our freedom, the forgiveness of our sins" (Eph 1:7).

Sinful Actions Come from the Rebellious Heart

Since the contemporary understanding of sin is so confused—confused to the point of denial that sin exists —

Christians need to turn to divine revelation to share in God's own understanding of sin. There can be no better source for us today, since God knows the innermost secrets of our hearts (cf. Heb 4:12-13).

The Book of Deuteronomy, a most ancient text[17] and one of the first five books of the Bible, sets before us two ways (cf. Dt. 30:15-20), as does Psalm 1. One way leads to life and prosperity and the other to death and disaster. The first requires obedience to the commandments of the Lord God. The second is the result of sin—straying from God's commands and refusing to listen to his teachings. The first way unites with divine holiness; the second way of sin separates humans from God.

Sin causes this violent split because all sin is rooted in hatred toward God and in rebellion against his commands (*CCC* 398, 415, 1487). Jesus described the basic attitude of the sinner when he said: "Men have shown they prefer darkness to the light because their deeds were evil" (Jn 3:19-21).

Sin, furthermore, is in the depths of the person's being; it is not just in the person's actions (*CCC* 705). All human actions flow from their roots deep in the human heart (*CCC* 2563), so although a person may appear "nice" or "respectable,"[18] if the person's actions result in harm to others or to himself or herself, that person's heart is evil. There is no other explanation for evil actions. Jesus said:

> It is from the human heart that evil intentions emerge: fornication, theft, murder, adultery, avarice, malice, deceit, indecency, envy, slander, pride, folly. All these evil things come from within and defile a person (Mk 7:20-23).

Sinners Make Their Own Hell

But scripture is even more perceptive about the true nature of sin and, therefore, the sinner's heart. It has to be admitted that it is difficult to reconcile the love God has for us with the heavy punishments in the gospel for sin, until we recognize the true evil of sin: hatred.[19] When we understand that, we are in a better position to appreciate the nature of God's holiness, and that the hatred of God from which the sinner acts is its own punishment. Hell is the consequence of the sinner's own free choice; it is the sinner's definitive self-exclusion from the presence of the most holy and loving God (*CCC* 1033).[20]

We have only to recall the growing hatred toward Jesus that is recounted in all four gospel accounts. This hatred cut his opponents off from Jesus, although Jesus would certainly welcomed them and forgiven them had they asked him to. But so deep in their hearts was their hatred of Jesus that it could only be satisfied by his death, and even then their hatred demanded the death of his followers. Jesus, knowing well the perversity of the human heart, prophesied to his disciples that the world would hate them because it hated him (cf. Jn 15:18–19).

When sin is rooted in the rebellious heart, the heart no longer mirrors the tranquil order of the original creation. The sinner seeks his or her own ends in direct, willful opposition to what God has ordained as part of his master plan of creation.[21]

The Rebellious Heart Has Evil Consequences

When we look at the evil effects of sin altogether, we see that sin has extensive consequences. Understanding the consequences should motivate the parish team to form in their parish a genuine desire to avoid sin in all its forms. The first and major consequence of sin is that sin harms the sinners themselves by hardening their hearts to evil. Secondly, sinners become enslaved to habits of sin and that in turn separates them from God and other human beings. Finally, sin does great harm to others.

The Mission of the Parish: Mercy and Reconciliation

The mission of the parish team does not end with revealing the effects of sin. The parish is the place where Jesus reaches out to sinners in compassionate love in order to reconcile them to himself. And the parish team members are the ones who prepare the soul of the parish for reconciliation, especially by preaching the mercy of God. Pope John Paul II writes:

> Conversion to God always consists in discovering his mercy, that is, in discovering that love which is patient and kind as only the Creator and Father can be; the love to which the God and Father of our Lord Jesus Christ is faithful to the uttermost consequences in the history of his covenant with man: even to the cross and to the death and resurrection of the Son. Conversion to God is always the fruit of the rediscovery of this Father, who is rich in mercy....Authentic knowledge of the God of mercy, the God of tender love, is a constant and inexhaustible source of conversion, not only as a momentary interior act but also as a permanent attitude, as a state of mind.[22]

Sin Leads to the Hardening of the Heart of the Sinner

Although the most evident and measurable effects of sin are in its social consequences, sin has profound, if more hidden, effects on the one who sins. The first and most serious effect sin has is that sin hardens the heart (CCC 1864). Sin blinds the sinner to the goodness of God "who gives the rain, the early rain and the later, at the right time of year, who assures us of weeks appointed for harvest" (cf. Jer 5:20-25).

The hardened heart grows increasingly insensitive to wrongdoing and increasingly alienated from God, the godly and the good. As the Book of Sirach says: "He who despises trifles will sink down little by little" (Sir 19:1). Another way of putting it is: "What starts small ends big." The small embezzlement done over a period of time results in a large embezzlement and great injustice.[23]

How common that is today. Those whose consciences have been deadened by sin focus on themselves and the turmoil caused by their uncontrolled passions; they lose the capacity to perceive the actions of God in the lives of others and, therefore, to see good in others. Not sensitive to the good in others, they are not able to respect others. Instead, they become judgmental and critical. Sin feeds their hatred for others, since hatred of God is the root of sin in the first place.

Consequently, in spite of high-sounding sentiments of sincerity, if the other person is weaker than the sinner, the sinner will take advantage of the other in terms of personal relationships such as friendship or certainly in business relations. On the other hand, it is more difficult to defraud someone you basically respect.

Sinners are like the Pharisees who accused Christ of getting his power from the demons (Mt 9:34). The Pharisees were blind to the manifest goodness in Christ, and, as a result, their hatred for him grew as they saw his holiness attracting the respect, admiration and awe of the crowds. This growing blindness and hatred, as the gospels attests, ultimately led to the crucifixion of Jesus and the subsequent bloody persecution of his followers.

Sin Enslaves and Alienates

In fact, while sin can give the impression of leading to real freedom, sin actually results in ever-deepening bondage to one's basest instincts of self-indulgence.[24]

Far from leading to personal satisfaction and fulfillment, sin is an act which results in behavior that causes personal shame (cf. Rom 6:21). The fallout from such behavior often overwhelms the sinner. Hating God, sinners begin to hate themselves and become dissatisfied with their own person. Having goals other than what their loving Father in his wisdom has set for them in the very nature of things, they find they have neither the power nor the wisdom to get what they want. No matter how skillful they are at competing, someone can always surpass them. The urge to compete leads to incredible hostility, and when they cannot meet their self-set goals, sinners become angry and frustrated. This soon gives way to self-pity.

Cutting themselves off from God and their fellow human beings results in a sense of alienation and loneliness which they often stifle in sexual excesses, drugs, alcohol and a life-style that is centered on providing for themselves all kinds of material comfort. If this fails them, many have turned to suicide.

Psalm 10 expresses in a beautiful, poetic manner the psychology of the sinner. It might seem an extreme description of what is behind the evil actions of which we are all to some extent both victims and perpetrators, but underneath all of his reasoning and planning his evil works, one sentiment is above them all: "There is no God! God forgets, he hides his face, he does not see all" (Ps 10:3-11).

But sinners always focus on themselves and their "problems." They do not focus on how they can share their God-given gifts with others. The passion from which sin flows so blinds the perceptions that sinners cannot see what damage their behavior will bring about to them. The evil may not be intended, but sin brings about its own fruits, and for these fruits the sinner is truly responsible.

The mother shooting up drugs may not intend to pass on addiction to her baby, but there are numerous cases on record where this has happened. The embezzler may not intend to destroy the savings of elderly investors, but embezzlements have weakened companies to the point of extinction, and the investors, many of them elderly, have lost everything. The teenager who is robbing his first convenience store for some spending money may not intend to kill anyone, and probably does not, but the newspapers are full of stories where killings and maimings of innocent people result.

Sin Leads to Spiritual Blindness

Furthermore, sin leads to spiritual blindness; it is walking in darkness, not the light of God's glory. Walking in darkness, of course, causes the sinner to stumble and eventually to fall.[25]

When the sinner is separated from the divine, all aspects of human life are distorted because the sinner has deliberately defaced the image of God in the human person. Emotions, mind and will no longer function in consonance; instead, they war against each other, creating disorder in place of harmony, tension in place of serenity. Paul laments the power and divisiveness of sin:

> The fact is, I know of nothing good living in me—living, that is, in my flesh—for though the will to do what is good is in me, the performance is not, so instead of doing the good things I want to do, I carry out the sinful things I do not want (Rom 7:18).[26]

Since the sinner's heart is estranged from God the source of life, the only possible effect is spiritual death. "The wages of sin is death" (Rom 6:23).

Sin Has Destroyed the Lives of Others[27]

Although sinful actions are the result of a greater or lesser degree of malice residing in the heart of an individual (and today we find it hard to accuse individuals of being personally responsible for malice), sinful actions have consequences that go far beyond the single individual. For example, when a husband and wife commit sins against each other—such as rash judgment, refusal to forgive, harboring grudges, inconsiderateness—these individual actions may evolve into such a way of life that the marriage breaks up. Sin, in other words, intrudes so deeply into the relationship that the marriage can no longer support the contentions of the two against each other, and the marriage ends in divorce.

And then what happens? The spouses are not the only ones to reap the results. There is more and more evidence being accumulated to show that children of divorce suffer severely in their development as human beings when either raised in a contentious atmosphere or raised by a single parent.[28] Thus, evil spreads itself beyond the sinner or sinners to embrace others in its sinister web.

Any sin has far-reaching effects. In this country, the instability of marriage is taking a tremendous toll on the stability of society itself. There are a rising number of problems stemming from a high divorce rate that are not limited to the psychological scars on the spouses, their children and other family members, such as grandparents. These are certainly the most personally painful, to be sure.

The prophet Amos was well aware of the social consequences of sin. At the time he was prophesying (c. 750 B.C.) in the Northern Kingdom of Israel, the leaders of the people were oppressing the poor and leading lives of wanton luxury. When we read the prophet Amos we learn that the leaders practiced slavery, indulged in incest, practiced idolatry and robbed the poor.[29]

As a result of this sinful behavior, the entire national spirit was being weakened. Amos saw, under the inspired movement of prophetic insight, that the country would not have the will or the strength to defend itself against a stronger and more resolute nation. Hence, Amos prophesied that the

Assyrians would conquer them and that all their wealth and luxuries would be destroyed. He viewed this as a punishment of God for sin (cf. Am 3:15).

God Permits the Consequences of Sin To Take Effect

Sin is a deliberate turning away from the Holy. Disobedience, a lack of trust, self- centeredness—all lead to alienation from the divine goodness and self-giving. Scripture clearly states the effects of sin.

In the Old Testament, before the clear development of the concept of the after-life, reward and punishment were seen as having to occur in the present existence. Therefore the prophets preached that Israel would be punished for its sins by political disasters—invasions by foreigners and exile.

Because the Israelites turned from God by putting their trust in Pharaoh instead of the Lord, Isaiah prophesied, "Pharaoh's protection will be your shame, the shelter of Egypt's shadow your confounding" (Is 30:3; 31:1-3). Saul lost his kingship because of his refusal to execute the ban against the Amalekites. "Obedience is better than sacrifice," Samuel told him (1 Sam 15:22).

While scripture teaches that God deeply desires the salvation of all, which is the very reason he sent his Son to rescue us from our sins, the text that perhaps most clearly expresses that will of God is carefully nuanced. The text is 1 Timothy 2:4:

> God wills that all be saved and come to a knowledge of the truth.

There are two parts to this text of equal importance. The first is the obvious statement that God wants to save all. The second part, however, describes how salvation is to be effected through grace, by coming to a knowledge of the truth. The truth is what saves. A person is "saved" when he or she walks in the light brought by Jesus Christ, or at least by the light of God's gift of reason (cf. Rom 2:14 ff.).

Salvation, then, is not automatic because Christ has come; salvation is effected when sinners turn from their sin and walk in the light of God's teaching. This walking in the light brings salvation now. By not walking in the light, human beings can freely choose to separate themselves from God's life-giving love, and not only in this life; they can freely choose to separate themselves from their loving Father even for all eternity, even as the Pharisees separated themselves from Jesus, the source of salvation. Such is the power God has given us in the great gift of free will.[30]

The Gospel of Matthew has numerous passages which refer to the final judgment and subsequent separation of the good from the evil, the former to everlasting joy and the latter to eternal punishment. As challenging as the task may be today, the parish team has the responsibility to teach what the gospel requires for holiness. We have choices, and our choices have consequences.[31]

The Gospel of Luke (Lk 10:17–24) emphasizes the heavenly reward awaiting those who become disciples of Jesus: "Rejoice that your names are written in heaven" (v. 20).[32]

Admission of Sin Is Required for Deliverance[33]

No matter how powerful sin is, or how powerful the temptation and allurement to do evil, the sinner is always responsible. Perhaps that is the greatest tragedy about sin. It seems irresistible when one is caught up in sin, yet one remains responsible for the sin and all its effects. Until ownership of the sin is accepted, deliverance from sin is not possible. The redeeming grace of Christ by which one is delivered from the slavery to sin requires first of all that the sinner acknowledge his or her sin.

When the Pharisees questioned Jesus' eating and drinking with tax collectors and sinners, Jesus responded: "I did not come to call the virtuous but sinners" (Mt 9:13)—sinners who knew they were sinners. The Gospel of John records Jesus' reply to the Pharisees when they refused to acknowledge their sinfulness.

The Pharisees said to Jesus:

> "Surely, we are not blind?" Jesus replied: "If you were blind, you would not be guilty; but since you say, 'We see,' your guilt remains" (Jn 9:41).

Scripture is filled with appeals for admission of guilt and reform of life. In the passage from the prophet Ezekiel we referred to earlier, God assured him that if the sinner renounces his sins and does what is lawful and right, he will be forgiven. If he makes restitution when he has stolen and if he keeps the commandments and stops committing sin, he shall live, and will not die. Even all his previous sins will no longer be remembered (Ez 33:14-16).

None of us can reform our lives by ourselves alone or on our own strength.[34] That is why Jesus came: to rescue us from the power of sin by sharing with us the power of his own love by which he overcame death on the cross. Even the power to call upon Jesus as savior is the effect of grace: "No one can say, 'Jesus is Lord,' unless he is under the influence of the Holy Spirit" (1 Cor 12:3). Hence, for the Christian the battle against sin is always a grace battle, fought with the weapons of Christic grace of which the parish team is the chosen instrument.[35]

The Battle Against Sin Requires Self-Discipline

Nevertheless, the nature of the battle requires constant self-discipline, since the Christian is called to imitate God himself.[36] Such self-discipline can be painful, but as the sinner turns from his or her sin and grows in holiness, the joy and peace of virtuous living in the Spirit soon supplant the passing pain of self-discipline. Self-discipline is part of carrying the cross. Jesus said to his disciples:

> If anyone wants to come after me, let him deny himself and take up his cross and follow me. For anyone who wants to save his life will lose it; but anyone who loses his life for my sake will find it (Mt 16:24–25).

And Paul adds: "You cannot belong to Christ Jesus unless you crucify all self-indulgent passions and lusts" (Gal 5:24).

While the Bible states that in some cases a sinner is subjected to physical suffering as a punishment for sin, not all physical suffering is punishment. On the contrary, when physical suffering is endured by the innocent, as Job suffered, the suffering is not punishment but an opportunity to grow in holiness. When Jesus was asked about a man blind from birth: "Who sinned, this man or his parents, for him to have been born blind?" Jesus responded, "He was born blind so that the works of God might be displayed in him" (Jn 9:2-3).

This kind of suffering is part of carrying the cross (cf. Phil 3:10).

There are many stories of people who have been seriously afflicted by disease or physical handicaps but have turned their distress into a blessing, both for themselves and for others. Furthermore, persecutions and martyrdoms have enriched the Church with canonized saints. The sin of the persecutors brought new and eternal life to their victims.

The earliest evidence for the value of martyrdom is found in the story of the mother and her seven sons in the

Second Book of Maccabees (7:1-42). In this story we have the first explicit expression of faith in the resurrection and eternal life. As the second son was dying he expressed this faith in his last words to his persecutor:

> With his last breath he exclaimed, "Inhuman monster, you may kill us, but the king of the world will raise us up, since it is for his laws that we die, to live again forever" (2 Mac 7:9).

The Book of Revelation calls for constancy in the face of persecution precisely because of the eternal reward it merits:

> Then I heard a voice from heaven say to me, "Write down: Happy are those who die in the Lord! Happy indeed, the Spirit says; now they can rest for ever after their work, since their good deeds go with them" (Rev 14:12-13).

The Task of the Parish Team

The parish team can be effective in preaching the hard truths about sin and the great evil it causes to both the sinner and others in the bright light of the saving truths of God's grace. At the same time, the church recognizes that holiness is a gift from our Father; it is a gift which is bestowed through the ministry of the church, and, therefore, through the ministry of the parish team. Nevertheless, to be able to accept the gift, we have to admit that we are not yet holy as God is holy. To help members of the parish come to that admission, the parish team needs to lead the parish to a thoughtful and heart-changing reflection on the life of holiness. This reflection, to be honest and useful, requires that the team preach about the generous gifts of grace that God gives to his children, along with practical ways of recognizing the harmful effects of sin in one's own life.

5

Holiness Is the Foundation of the Moral Law

Morality Is the Mystery of God's Action

*T*he Christian vocation is at root a call to holiness. Nothing we do has any lasting value for us unless it leads us to holiness: holiness for ourselves and holiness for others. Jesus said:

> What does it profit a man to gain the whole world and suffer the loss of his soul? (Lk 9:25).

The call to holiness is sometimes most vivid when we are not explicitly striving to accomplish great things, even for the Lord. The call to holiness sounds most powerfully in the everyday, ordinary affairs of our life when our conscience keeps us from doing evil and guides us into the paths of justice and right action.

Therefore, morality is not just about the externals of human behavior, but about their deepest source: the human heart. The laws of God, both those revealed and those as they exist in nature, are gifts that regulate the innermost movements of our hearts, which, in turn, direct our every external action so that we live wisely and in peace. Ultimately, the parish team members reveal the mystery of God's guiding action in the world when they teach the good news of

Catholic morality to the entire parish. The psalmist praises God's law when he says:

> Your decrees are so wonderful,
>   my soul cannot but respect them.
> As your work unfolds, it gives light,
>   and the simple understand (Ps 119:129–130).

Furthermore, when the word we have heard enables us to overcome our sinful inclinations, we experience the power of God at work in us and recognize the great unity to which he has called us—both to himself and to one another in love.

In Forgiving, We Experience the Goodness of God

Consider how this is verified in the proclamation of the command to forgive one another. The parish is the most effective setting in the whole world to proclaim forgiveness. It is truly the abode of reconciliation. Yet the injunction to forgive is not just a way to act; it reveals something of the nature of God's own wisdom. Unlike our human wisdom, God's wisdom is perfectly capable of judging, judging justly, and, most of all, judging mercifully—something which we, with our limited vision, can never do.

When we mirror the forgiveness of God, we learn experientially of the goodness of God; we participate in his own wisdom, which implies God's rectitude, since God always judges justly. For the parish team to preach forgiveness, therefore, is to enable the parish as a whole to enter into the mystery of God's power. To preach forgiveness is to proclaim the unity of people and to affirm the oneness of creation. To preach forgiveness is to announce the purification of the individual, who can now be united with the divine. The preaching of forgiveness can actually lead believers to a kind of ecstasy: those who forgive are drawn out of themselves.

In forgiving, the believer hands the justice of his cause over to the all-knowing and all-loving God. The word of God delivers the hearers from the limitations of their concept of justice by uniting them with the divine wisdom, justice and love. In this union with the divine, believers are able to experience a profound sense of true freedom because they have the surest sign that their own sins have been forgiven. Jesus says:

> Be compassionate as your Father is compassionate. Do not judge and you will not be judged yourselves; do not condemn and you will not be condemned yourselves; forgive and you will be forgiven (Lk 6:36-37).

The Parish Team Proclaims the Wisdom of the Law of God

Eternal wisdom insofar as it is the norm of action for human beings is called "law,"[1] and human beings are united to the Holy and participate in the divine holiness only when they obey the will of God by living according to his eternal wisdom. Jesus said:

> It is not those who say to me, "Lord, Lord," who will enter the kingdom of heaven, but the person who does the will of my Father in heaven (Mt 7:21).

Kinds of Law

The Eternal Law

The *eternal law* as the term is used in theology exists in God himself and is the divine wisdom eternally directing the movements and activities of all things to their proper ends.[2] All other laws are derived from the eternal law, including human laws insofar as they are in conformity with right reason.[3]

The Natural Law

The *natural law,* although it participates in the eternal law, has not been the fruit of a special divine revelation. It is not a revealed law. It has been implanted in the hearts of all human beings by the Creator who made us, so that by an instinct of right reason itself all human beings will be able to act in a way that leads to their personal happiness and communal peace.[4]

Because the natural law has never been written out, like revealed law, it depends very much on the diverse understanding of what is "natural" or "in accord with nature."[5] We see that conflict today in the public policy disputes that are an integral part of making new laws in the United States. Nevertheless, there are some principles of the natural law that are quite clear; in fact, St. Paul considers that the existence of God, a fundamental principle of the natural law, is so evident from nature itself that even those who do not know God through revelation are accountable for not living by the consequences of God's existence:

> What can be known about God is manifest to them [nonbelievers], for God himself has manifested it...in the things that he created...Instead they did not think reasonably, and their heart was darkened (Rom 1:18–32).

God created humanity good, as Genesis teaches, and by nature the human person tends to the good and not to evil. Our human nature images the divine.[6] Tragically, from the original sin to the sins of our own day, our natural tendency to the good has been seriously weakened so that we have to struggle to overcome selfishness. Therefore, Paul, in the passage cited above, goes on to describe the downward moral spiral that results from our not acknowledging God and praising him. It is a description of our times.

Pagans Have a Limited Power To Live by the Natural Law[7]

Pagans[8] do not have the clear revelation of the divine law that comes through faith, but they do have the natural law imprinted in all human beings; it is the substance of the revealed law written in their hearts by their Creator. When, therefore, they live in obedience to that law by following the right judgments of their own conscience, they are able to know right from wrong, and, by living rightly, to be pleasing to God (cf. Rom 2:12-16).

In his audience of September 9, 1998, Pope John Paul II reaffirmed this teaching of the church:

> It must first be kept in mind that every quest of the human spirit for truth and goodness, and in the last analysis for God, is inspired by the Holy Spirit. The various religions arose precisely from this primordial human openness to God. At their origins we often find founders who, with the help of God's Spirit, achieved a deeper religious experience. Handed on to others, this experience took form in the doctrines, rites and precepts of the various religions.[9]

The Bible appreciates the complexity of knowing the natural law and being able to live by it. The Book of Wisdom is quite understanding of those human beings who have not received the explicit revelation given in the Old Testament. It does not condemn them outright; rather, it emphasizes the difficulty of coming to accurate knowledge about God. The fact is that the beauty of the things God has made is very attractive in itself, and searchers after God can be led astray—resting content with the creature rather than going on to seek the Creator. Nevertheless, they cannot be completely excused; since they are intelligent enough to be able to explore the creation, they should be able to arrive at the Creator of such beauty (cf. Wis 13:6-9).

Humans Cannot Judge the Human Heart

Such an appreciation of the difficulty of coming to a clear knowledge of what is right or wrong, what is sinful or not, has important ramifications for Christians today.[10]

The Christian gospel does not teach Christians to go about denouncing people because they do not acknowledge the revelation given to us by the gift of God, nor can they arbitrarily say non-believers are going to hell. Christians cannot divide the world into the saved and the unsaved, the chosen and the reprobates. No human being has enough information about the human heart to judge it (cf. Rom 2:12-16). Jesus himself said:

> Do not judge and you will not be judged yourselves; do not condemn, and you will not be condemned yourselves; grant pardon, and you will be pardoned (Lk 6:37).

Yet this tendency to quick judgment has always been a great temptation among the devout, who sometimes forget that the ultimate judgment of a person is strictly God's business—one about which God is very jealous.[11] Paul, addressing the controversy in the early church about eating meat sacrificed to idols, wrote:

> It is not for you to judge someone else's servant: to his own master, he stands or falls; he will stand, you may be sure, because the Lord has the power to make him stand (Rom 14:4).

The ultimate question is not whether one has observed all the precepts of religious law (which may not be divine),[12] but whether or not one has loved. All of the precepts of the natural law as well as divine law are fulfilled when human beings—believers or non-believers—love their neighbors. "If you love your fellow human beings, you have fulfilled the law" (Rom 13:8).[13]

The Divine Law[14]

Given the ambiguity of the natural law, it is not surprising that God, in his hunger to unite us with himself, revealed in more explicit terms those principles of human behavior that would lead all human beings into union with him through holiness. This explicit revelation is called the *divine law*. It, too, like the natural law, is an external expression of the eternal law. Divine law is the revealed law of God directing all human beings to their proper and supernatural end.

Divine law, however, differs significantly from human law in one essential aspect: divine law is not imposed arbitrarily by the power of God, as some human laws are; divine law is not an expression of God's will as if God were the boss demanding service and submission.[15] In the earlier stages of revelation, the emphasis was more on "God's will" than God's wisdom. Through the stages of revelation, however, law as wisdom and light is more prominent. Even in the Old Testament God's law is God's loving wisdom guiding us to happiness both on earth and in heaven. For this reason the psalmist prays:

> Happy those who respect his decrees,
>   and seek him with their whole heart,
> and who do no evil,
>   but walk in his ways (Ps 119:2-3).

The Divine Law Was Revealed First in the Old Law[16]

The divine law was promulgated by God first and imperfectly through Moses and the prophets and the religious traditions of the Hebrews, Israelites and Jews. Because this teaching is found in the Old Testament, we Christians call this divine law the old law. The old law was concerned with ordering human activities to obtain the material and terrestrial good of the Hebrew people.

The minute observances of the old law in matters of ritual, eating, drinking and clothing, as well as regarding the larger matters of interpersonal relationships and justice, were all intended to make God present to the community in the largest and smallest actions of life. God was not only aware of one's activities when they were in conformity to his expressed will and pleasure, God was actively and lovingly involved in them. On the other hand, failure to follow the divine commands would lead to severe *consequences*.[17]

Chapters 17–26 in the Book of Leviticus constitute the "holiness code." It consists of a multitude of injunctions regulating the most intimate and personal human actions, many of them having to do with sexual relations. The point of this code and other laws of holiness is to stress that in order to draw close to God—the Holy, Transcendent One—the individual must be ritually clean; that is, prepared in mind and body to take part in the community's worship.[18] This understanding was refined as revelation unfolded through the prophets and the New Testament. Ritual purity was the preparation for the spiritual purity and moral integrity demanded and made possible by the saving gospel of Jesus Christ.

The Divine Law Was Revealed in the New Law of Christ

The divine law is also revealed in the gospel and is called the new law of Christ.[19] Both the old law and the new law are revelatory of the will and wisdom of God, but there is a basic difference between them.[20] The old law only tells us what is wrong—an important revelation in itself; the new law gives us the power to do something about it. For this reason, Paul calls the Law of Moses the law of sin and death (cf. Rom 3:20).

While the old law reveals what is sinful without giving us the power to comply with it, the new law has the power to make the sinner holy because the new law is the grace of the Holy Spirit, which is given through faith in Christ.[21] The Gospel of Matthew presents Jesus as the new Moses giving the new law. In the Sermon on the Mount Jesus says:

> Do not imagine that I have come to abolish the [old] law or the prophets. I have come not to abolish them but to bring them to completion (Mt 5:17).

Jesus' new law orders human actions so that all who obey the new law through faith can enter into the heavenly kingdom. When Jesus gave his disciples the new law, Jesus told them: "The words I have spoken to you are spirit and they are life" (Jn 6:63).

The New Testament is concerned with the acts and experiences which enable the faithful reader to attain to the grace of the Holy Spirit. The new law is communicated through the preaching of Jesus and the writings of the New Testament consequent upon his preaching. The sacred writings of the New Testament either dispose their readers for accepting this grace or teach them how to use it.[22] Knowledge of the law is not enough. In order to achieve holiness through union with the Divine, we need the power to obey the law, a capacity which comes to us through the grace of Christ. When Christ was crucified and died on the cross, he won reconciliation with God and forgiveness of sin through faith (cf. Rom 3:21–26).

The entire Chapter 8 of the Letter to the Romans is an inspiring teaching on the power of the new law: the law of the spirit of life in Christ Jesus has set us free from the law of sin and death because we have been made just by Jesus Christ. In other words, the grace of Christ has entered into the very depths of our soul and made us holy, not because of our merits, but simply because God has willed Christ to be our Savior (cf. Rom 8). We can be totally united to the Holy only through the action and wisdom of God himself.

As Psalm 143 puts it: "Lord, no one is virtuous by your standard" (Ps 143:2).

The Parish Team Are Ambassadors for Christ

Our need to know and obey the divine law in order to become holy is evident from the fact that we human beings frequently err in making judgments about the right things we should do and the evil things we should avoid. This is due to two causes: we have limited knowledge, and the circumstances of our lives are constantly changing.

What may seem to be good in one circumstance is seen to be harmful in another. (To give money to a poor person to help pay the rent is good; to give to someone equally poor who we know will use it to get drunk is bad.) We are pulled between conflicting values, and repeatedly we find we just do not have enough information to make proper decisions leading us to holiness.

Consequently, when homilists, catechists, evangelists, parents, all of whom share in some way in the church's ministry of the word, communicate the divine law as revealed by Jesus Christ, they communicate both the wisdom and the strength to be holy and to enjoy the fruits of holiness: namely, peace and joy. They say: "This is how grace works." To put the parish team ministry today in terms Paul uses in his Second Letter to the Corinthians, the parish team is made up of ambassadors for Christ. God is appealing through the team for their listeners to be reconciled to God, and thereby become holy as God is holy (cf. 2 Cor 5:17-21).

The Law Reveals Sin

With the revelation of the divine law in both the Old and New Testaments we have the revelation of sin as an offense against the very holiness of God as he directs all things to their proper ends according to his eternal and loving wisdom—the eternal law.[23] Sin, interior dispositions and attitudes, as well as exterior actions or omissions, therefore, can be identified precisely as offenses against the eternal law only through a revelation by faith.

Without revelation, a person may experience deep unhappiness and frustration; his or her selfishness may even do great harm to others. Nevertheless the person may not realize that these painful experiences and hurtful actions are the result of being separated from God's holy wisdom through personal sin. It is only after the acceptance of revelation and the consequent conversion of heart that the believer recognizes personal sin as the cause of this previous situation. A common experience of people who have reformed their lives is a sense of shame and regret for what they were. They recognize that their former way of life was unworthy of them, and, as Paul says, they blush as they recall the painful past (Rom 6:20-21).

The Letter to the Ephesians puts it even more strongly. It says that those who do not live in holiness through obedience to the divine law are instead enslaved to their own lusts. As a result, they are forced to follow their illusions (really delusions) about what will bring them happiness (cf. Eph 2:3).

Since holiness requires that the human heart have the right desires, divine law—that is, revealed law—does not limit itself to regulating only external actions, as does human law. Whereas human law is concerned exclusively with directing actions that affect others in the community, divine law provides practical norms of action to guide the development of the very core of the human person. Only divine law has the competency to do that; only the divine law is extensive and perceptive enough to reveal what is sinful in the cravings of the human heart.[24]

The great prophet of the Old Testament, Jeremiah, was personally very familiar with the twists and turns the human heart can take in its pursuit of evil. So twisted is the human heart that only God can search the heart, judge it, and give to each person what his or her works deserve.[25]

Communicating the Divine Law Makes God Present

Thus, it is clear from scripture itself that when the parish team communicates the divine law revealed in the gospel, they are giving more than good advice or imposing exalted goals that are difficult to achieve. They are giving more than information about morality. The team is always proclaiming good news of salvation.

Of course, the communication of Catholic morality does inform the minds of the listeners as to what is right and wrong, acceptable and unacceptable to God, and helpful or harmful to their relationships with their fellow human beings.

Still, Catholic moral preaching is more. Preaching the moral law in the Spirit of Christ actually enables the listeners to experience the active presence and power of the transcendent God in their lives here and now in all of their daily activities and their most trivial actions. The word of God they proclaim is a word of power that effects what it proclaims. The divine word is not just an exhortation to try harder; it gives birth to new life and confers new power.

> Your new birth was...from the everlasting word of the living and eternal God....What is this word? It is the good news that has been brought to you (1 Pt 1:23-25).

Thus, through the keeping of the moral law we learn by actually doing good the true nature of the kingdom of God. When we experience joy and peace even in the midst of intense physical suffering and mental anguish, we know that the gospel promises are true. When we live according to the law of the gospel we become vividly aware that we are sharing in the wisdom of God Most High.

Guilt Is Often a Personal Revelation of the Moral Law

We have seen that God reveals his will and presence to us through both human reason and divine revelation. When believers obey the law of Christ and non-believers follow their consciences the best they can, God manifests his presence by making us immediately aware of his pleasure in us through the presence of the Holy Spirit in our hearts.

Paul describes the vivid Christian experience thus:

> The proof that you are children of God is that God has sent the Spirit of his Son into our hearts: the Spirit that cries, "Abba, Father," and it is this that makes you his child. You are not a slave anymore; and if God has made you his child, then he has made you an heir (Gal 4:6-7).

God also speaks to us very powerfully through a guilty conscience. Some today look upon feeling guilty as an evil to be avoided. Many have spent a great deal of money trying to escape from a pervading sense of guilt. When guilt has no specific object, that is, when someone feels guilty but does not know the cause of the emotion, guilt can degenerate into energy-sapping anxiety and anguish. Anxiety will never lead to any positive reform of life; indeed it only makes the finding of the "authentic" self more difficult.[26]

There is also neurotic or scrupulous guilt when persons are tormented by feelings of guilt for actions which common sense tells them are not sins, or for accidents for which they were not really responsible.

Real guilt, however, results from real sin which we knowingly and freely commit, and no psychotherapy can remove this guilt. To remove this guilt and feelings accompanying it requires repentance, reparation, and forgiveness of God, as well as the forgiveness of those whom we have injured.

In the Christian spiritual life, however, conscience is precisely the point where divine grace enters powerfully into human judgments about what to do in order to act in union with divine wisdom.[27] Being chosen means that the sinner is delivered from sin and the evils that result from it. Frequently, the most powerful voice announcing the divine choice is the voice of conscience that clearly and unmistakably tells us when we are doing evil and separating ourselves from the holiness of God. God speaks to us individually through our conscience, and there he speaks powerfully. An awareness of having committed a serious wrong—a real sin—has led many to a profound conversion of life and a deep and lasting union with the Lord. The first words of Jesus in the Gospel of Mark were a call to conversion and repentance of sins: "The time has come, and the kingdom of God is close at hand. Repent, and believe the good news" (Mk 1:15).

For example, many today commit vicious crimes against their fellow human beings: rape, murder, theft. Some of these crimes are simply born out of the passing passion of the moment: angry enough to kill, sexually aroused enough to rape, greedy enough to steal.

Some of these crimes find their roots in the way the perpetrator was brought up—by abusive parents, for example. Other crimes, some recent studies are beginning to purport, are the result of genetically influenced behavior. Still others are committed by persons who seem to have some tragic flaw within them which leads them to sinful actions that eventually bring about their own destruction. This is a reality that the Greek tragedies, such as *Oedipus*, explored as a powerful theme in portraying the perplexing matters of the human heart.

Deliverance from even the desire to murder, rape, steal—or indeed any form of evil—is a totally free gift from a merciful God who holds us close to himself in an embrace of endless love. As a result, we praise God for the glory of his grace (Eph 1:3-7).

Grace Leads to Virtue and a Way of Life[28]

So powerful is the movement of grace that it enables us to act righteously on a constant, habitual basis. We realize that we are truly acting in a way that so exceeds our own natural powers that we call it salvation. The holy person recognizes that his holiness, justice and wisdom is not his or her own, but indeed a gift from God. Awareness of being so generously gifted, in turn, gives us a sense of vocation, a sense of being called to a higher life by the Father who loves us. Because of God's call to receive his gifts, we can then govern our lives through the particularity of the innumerable specific choices we have to make with regard to family, job and self.[29]

The Parish Calls God's People to Repentance

When we do something wrong, guilt lets us know what God wants us to do, and the way to get rid of that guilty feeling is not to rationalize our sinful actions or let someone talk us out of the feeling. The only Catholic way to remove the experience of legitimate guilt[30] in serious matters is to receive the sacrament of reconciliation and avoid the sinful action in the future (CCC 1446). Thus living by one's conscience when it is properly formed through gospel teaching reveals God's personal will for us in a very unique and specific way.

We Are Called to Unity in Holiness

When the forceful movement of God's grace gives us the power to overcome our sinful inclinations, we recognize the great unity to which he has called us: We are to be one in holiness with him and one another in love. Living in harmony with God's will, we experience a true sense of inner peace and find ourselves in harmony with other human beings and indeed with all of nature because God has made his home in our hearts and lives (Jn 14:21-23).

The parish team can transform a parish when it constantly and faithfully teaches this good news.

6

Holiness Makes Family Life a Real Joy

*P*eople are hungry for love. They want to love and be loved. The use of such common catchwords such as "sharing," "community," and "support" are expressive of this yearning. Given this hunger for love, the parish team has an audience ready to listen to the good news of the Catholic teaching on human love. True love leads to holiness and the joy it brings.

Christian Love Is Divine Love in the Flesh

Since we are made in the image and likeness of God, graced human love is a participation in divine love. Jesus commands his disciples to express his love for them in their love for one another. Active love is a witness to Jesus' love and, in turn, will become a prototype for everyone to love others; therefore, when we love from the depths of our heart, we love as God does (Jn 13:34-35). When Paul describes the qualities of love in his First Letter to the Corinthians, he is in reality describing how we show forth divine love in our treatment of others: patient, kind, never rude or selfish. "[Love] is always ready to excuse, to trust, to hope and to endure all things. Love never ends" (1 Cor 13:1-7).

While God calls all Christians to love one another, the sacrament of marriage gives married couples the power to embody the love of Jesus in an enduring way in every aspect of their lives, including the biological: the way they treat one another with kindness, patience, consideration; the way they treat their children with the respect due them as persons; the way they take care in teaching them; the way they present themselves as models for them. This is their witness to Jesus in the world, and their witness brings light to the world.

Pope Paul VI said:

> The very manifestations of the tenderness of Christian spouses are permeated with this love which they draw from the heart of God. And should the human source happen to dry up, the divine source is as inexhaustible as the fathomless depths of the tenderness of God. This reveals to what an intimate, strong and rich communion conjugal love tends. As an interior and spiritual reality, it transforms the community life of the spouses into what we could call, according to the authorized teaching of the council: "the domestic Church."[1]

Furthermore, in the sacred art and act of marital love, a husband and wife become procreators with God himself of new human life. The person they beget with God is not destined for this world alone. They bring into existence a child who is made for the joys of heaven in holy union with the Father through Jesus Christ in the Holy Spirit.

The first chapter of the first book of the Bible, the Book of Genesis, relates how God, immediately after having created the first man and woman in his own image and likeness, commands them to be the givers of life to others:

> God blessed them, saying to them, "Be fruitful, multiply, fill the earth and conquer it" (Gen 1:28).

After giving life, God continues to protect it and foster it. Life is the first and most basic contact human persons have with the holiness of their creator. For this reason, a large part of scripture is focused on God's providential care of his people of the Old Testament in all their victories and all their defeats. God is always with them and active, to both reward and punish. His providence is the mark of his holiness.

The Old Testament Reveals the Purpose of Human Life[2]

The Old Testament reveals the purpose of human life in this world: to live in conformity with God's will and, for the chosen people, to obey his statutes.[3] The happiness resulting from this conformity to the divine holiness is defined in terms of large numbers of descendants, good harvests, and deliverance from enemies.

In fact, the historical books of the Old Testament, which constitute a significant portion of the Hebrew Bible, are concerned with the events in the people's history that show their relationship to God at any given time. When the Israelites obey him and are faithful to the covenant he enjoined upon them through Moses, they are blessed. When they wander from his teachings, they are punished. But the relationship with God is explored only in terms of this life on earth, and holiness is objectified to a great extent by detailed demands for ritual cleanliness.[4]

The New Testament Explicitly Reveals That Human Life Never Ends

Because the New Testament develops the theme of God's power and intention to give, promote and protect life, it bolsters scripture's understanding of the holiness of life. The prologue to the Gospel of John begins by identifying the Word first of all as the giver of human life. Furthermore, God has created human beings and given them life so that they might acquire knowledge and understanding of God in a world that exists in darkness. To know God, to live in his love according to his commands, is to live in the light, a basic theme of the entire Gospel of John (cf. Jn 1:1-5).

By the time Jesus was born, a large number of Jews believed that human life was eternal; it was also the teaching of the Pharisees. Still, there were some Jews who rejected that teaching. The Sadducees, mainly Jewish priests, taught that life ended with the grave, and they argued with Jesus about it, ridiculing his affirmation of the resurrection.[5]

Jesus explained to them that human life never comes to an end; it goes on beyond death itself. Appealing to the Old Testament, he said to them:

> Have you never read what God said to you: "I am the God of Abraham, the God of Isaac and the God of Jacob"? God is not God of the dead, but of the living (Mt 22:31-32).

In his exchanges with the Sadducees, Jesus gives us a brief but impressive insight into the manner of human existence for all eternity. Jesus said:

> Those who are judged worthy of a place in the other world and in the resurrection from the dead do not marry because they can no longer die, for they are the same as the angels, and being children of the resurrection, they are sons of God (Lk 20:35-36).

The resurrection of the dead is a fundamental doctrine of the Christian faith, and with belief in the resurrection comes a richer appreciation of the purpose of human life. Jesus teaches us that human beings are not made simply to live and die on earth. From the moment of our beginning we have an eternal destiny. God created us to live with our Father forever in the kingdom of his beloved Son, Jesus. Paul writes: "Just as all die in Adam, so all will be brought to life in Christ" (1 Cor 15:22).

Holiness Now Is Forever in Glory

Holiness, then, is more than ritual cleanliness and even right living; holiness on earth is preparation for eternal holiness—a union of joy and peace with God in the heavenly kingdom. Holiness now is a foretaste of the glories that are to come which the Book of Revelation describes in a magnificent vision of the New Jerusalem when God will "wipe away all tears from their eyes; there will be no more death, and no more mourning or sadness. The world of the past has gone" (Rev 21:3-4).

Moreover, the New Testament underscores God's universal care of all human life, even that beyond the Jewish nation. Within this universal concern, however, the New Testament concentrates especially on the life of persons who are united to the Father through faith in his Son.

The revelation of this eternal dimension gives Christians a unique, clear perspective on the value of life in this world: *life is given for humans to become holy and so to be united to the Father forever in his eternal kingdom.*

The Quality of Life Is Judged Only by Holiness

Since human life never ends, the quality of life cannot be judged rightly by many of the standards of modern secular society. Because a person is badly crippled or dying of incurable cancer does not mean that the quality of that human life has been lessened. Especially, it does not mean that the quality of life has been lessened to the extent that it should be destroyed.

Life in this world is preparation for the life yet to come, and hence all things enhance human life if the person's reaction to the things that happen to him or her lead the person to holiness. As a matter of fact, suffering may actually improve the quality of human life because of the way it is endured.

No matter how great the suffering in this life, the Father knows every detail of it. When the sufferer bears it patiently in union with Christ on his cross, the suffering will improve the quality of life in eternity. Paul writes to the Romans: "I think that what we suffer now can never be compared to the glory that is to come" (Rom 8:18).

As a result of Jesus' revelation of life beyond the grave, the New Testament gives believers today a new perspective by which to judge the mysteries of human life that only confounded Job. For example, what great injustices persecutors have worked against Christians and what great sufferings they have caused them! Nevertheless, Jesus said:

> Do not be afraid of those who kill the body but cannot kill the soul....Are not two sparrows sold for a penny? And yet not one falls to earth without your Father's knowledge. Even the hairs on your head are all numbered. Therefore, do not be afraid; you are worth more than many sparrows (Mt 10:28-31).

Sexual Love Is a Holy Gift From a Loving Father

With exceptions only in the lower plants and animals, all life is sexual, requiring a male and a female to create new life. Consequently, in shaping the spirituality of the parish the parish team cannot regard God's gift of sexuality as primarily a danger to be carefully avoided. This attitude should not exist because sex is at the core of life. The good news is that

God has redeemed humankind and made sex holy. That is good news indeed.

The Bible emphasizes the dignity of the human person made in the image and likeness of God. The underlying principle regulating all human sexual relations in the Bible is that sex between spouses communicates life and love similar to the life and love in the Most Holy Trinity, and because life and love are holy, the sexual act of communicating human life and love is also holy.

The Song of Songs is perhaps the most captivating expression of love in the Bible. In spite of its sensual, even erotic nature, the Song of Songs has always been accepted into the canon of inspired scripture.[6] Although it has been variously interpreted over the centuries as an allegory of human relations with the divine, to the ordinary reader of faith it also remains a stirring poem in praise of marital love. Like similar love poems its focus is on the romantic emotions love engenders. Although it has a mystical meaning, the Song of Songs is first a literal model of scripture's reverence for the spouses' passion for one another.

> On my bed, at night, I searched for him
>   whom my heart loves....
> When I found him whom my heart loves,
>   I held on to him; I would not let him go (Sg 3:1-4).

To protect the holiness of his gift of sexuality to his children, our Father has surrounded human sexual life with clear commands. By incorporating and making the wisdom of these commands their own, husbands and wives can achieve deeper union with one another and with God through their love for one another in its total human expression, which includes necessarily sexual expression. Union brings joy, so the Book of Proverbs urges a man to find joy in his wife:

> Find joy with the wife you married in your youth beauti-
> ful as a deer, graceful as a fawn. Let her breasts satisfy
> you at all times; be exhilarated always with her love (Prov
> 5:18-19).

Conjugal Relations Can Bring
Married Persons Closer to God

Because human beings are sexual persons, authentic sexual activity in marriage affects the bodies of the spouses and it
perfects them as persons.[7] The apostle Paul teaches that the
body is the temple of the Holy Spirit, and, therefore, we should
use our body only to give God glory (cf. 1 Cor 6:18-20).
Accordingly, when anyone—married or single—acts virtuously
in matters of sex, this behavior builds up a relation with God.
Consequently, the Bible treats sex in considerable detail.
Virtuous sexual relations in marriage effect a more intimate
union with God for the couple, because the sexual act unites
husband and wife in holy love, and in that act of holy love they
are able beget children in their own image and in the image and
likeness of God. They beget children who are destined to live
forever in the glory of the Father with the Son and Holy Spirit.

The Law of Holiness

The most ancient tradition in divine revelation regarding
the holiness of sex is found in the Book of Leviticus in the law
of holiness. A single, very positive command forms the basic
principle governing the detailed legislation that protects the
holiness of sexual activity:

> You must make yourselves holy, for I am Yahweh your
> God. You must keep my laws and put them into practice,
> for it is I, Yahweh, who make you holy (Lv 20:7-8).

There then follows a long list (vv. 9-21) of laws describing how the holiness of God and the holiness of sex can be violated by certain sexual practices. All of these practices ultimately in some way violate the holiness of the family by turning sexual acts away from engendering legitimate blood relations. To put it another way, the marriage act must always be open to the creation of new life for the family. In *Humanae Vitae,* Pope Paul VI warned against the consequences of a contraceptive mentality: conjugal infidelity, the denigration of women and the intervention of public authority in the prevention of birth among the "undesirables" in a population.[8]

Jesus himself reaffirms the validity of the law of holiness. He did not come to abolish the law or the prophets. When he came on earth, his teaching brought the law to its perfect conclusion and the achievement of its purpose—to lead us to holiness (cf. Mt 5:17-18). In fact, he raises the requirements for sexual purity to a higher level of holiness than the earlier more primitive and less developed codes:

> You have learned how it was said: You must not commit adultery. But I say this to you: if a man looks at a woman with lust, he has already committed adultery with her in his heart (Mt 5:27-28).

Because the law of holiness regarding sexual activity is so basic, its regulations can never be abrogated or modified. Other laws may be lessened as a result of new circumstances—for example, the prohibition against usury—but no cultural situation can alter the way human life is passed on through the generations.

The New Testament further develops this basic understanding. The apostle Paul teaches that in marriage, the spouses surrender their rights over their own bodies to one another for the other's exclusive use.

> Let each man have his own wife and each woman her
> own husband. The husband must give his wife her due,
> and so too the wife to the husband. The wife has no
> rights over her own body; her husband has them. In the
> same way, the husband has no rights over his body; the
> wife has them (1 Cor 7:2-4).

At the same time, the exercise of these rights or the
refusal to exercise them is governed by the couple's need to
grow in holiness.

> Do not deprive each other except by mutual agreement,
> and then only for a time, to devote yourselves to prayer;
> then come together again in case Satan should tempt you
> because of a lack of self-control (1 Cor 7:5).

The strictures against fornication and adultery in scripture which protect sexual holiness, therefore, are opposed to
widely-tolerated, if not actually approved, social customs of
Paul's own times among the Greeks.

The parish team will contribute greatly to the improvement
in the stability of the family in our world today, where the divorce
rate is so tragically high, when it forms the parish in a positive
and biblical attitude regarding the holiness of the human body
as the temple of the Holy Spirit and all the actions of the human
person as manifestations of the divine life within us.

The Sacramental Marriage Bond Is Holy
and Leads to Holiness[9]

The Bible views marriage as the only legitimate exercise
of the sexual act, and both Old and New Testaments strongly
forbid extramarital activity. The form of marriage has varied in
the Old Testament: polygamy, monogamy (this being the preferred form without doubt), and levirate.[10] The New
Testament allows only monogamy, and marriage is to take

place only between Christians, although some exceptions are permitted with non-Christians.[11]

While biblical literature extols three aspects of marriage relationship between spouses—the personal, the spiritual, and companionship—marriage has yet another function: it establishes covenantal relationships between families. Clearly this last effect is not as evident in modern culture as it has been in the past when religion and inheritance rights of clans and families were important issues. In the Book of Tobit, for example, Tobit gave his son Tobiah a series of admonitions to insure that his clan would flourish, and the choice of the right wife for him was essential to the future health of his society. He said:

> Choose a wife of your father's lineage. Do not take a foreign wife outside your father's tribe, because we are the sons of the prophets. Remember Noah, Abraham, Isaac and Jacob, our fathers from the beginning. All of them took wives from their own kindred, and they were blessed in their children, and their descendants will inherit the earth (Tb 4:12).

After the return from the exile the prophet Nehemiah vehemently condemned those Jews who had married non-Jewish women:

> I upbraided them and cursed them;...They were traitors to our God by marrying foreign women (cf. Neh 13:23-27).

Up until quite recent times, the destinies of the nations of Europe were frequently settled by intermarriages among the ruling families. For example, the great and extensive Austro-Hungarian Empire was built not through war, as many empires were built, but through marriages. The Hapsburgs arranged marriages with the ruling families of Flanders, Burgundy, Spain, Trieste, Styria, Southern Tyrol, Netherlands, Bohemia and Hungary.

The Marriage Covenant Rests
on the Promise of the Spouses[12]

The marriage covenant, like all covenants, is based on the faithfulness of the covenanters to their word, which should be unbreakable. To put it another way, a marriage depends completely on the spouses' word of promise to one another. When they break their word and are not faithful to the implementation of that word in the practical decisions of married life, the marriage begins to weaken and sometimes completely fails.

The prophet Malachi prophesying after the rebuilding of the temple following the return from exile (c. 450 B.C.), answers the question, "Why does Yahweh refuse to accept our offerings?" The answer was because divorce had become an acceptable custom, whereas God says: "I hate divorce."[13]

Furthermore, true love is of its nature endless and unbreakable. A husband cannot promise to love his wife for only five years or ten; nor can a mother promise to raise her children in love for eighteen years and then stop loving them.

Faithfulness Comes From the Wellspring
of Unending Love[14]

In the Old Testament, the Book of Hosea recounts how God commands the prophet Hosea to marry Gomer, a prostitute. After Gomer begets children by him, she continues her adultery and is denounced by Hosea. Later, God commands him to take her back. This tragic marriage is a symbol of God's relations with his people Israel who have gone whoring after foreign gods, but whom God seeks out again and restores to his favor because of his love and his faithfulness. It is a symbol for us of the nature of faithful love, human as well as divine (cf. Hos 1-3).

The Letter to the Ephesians is the most explicit statement in the New Testament of the covenantal-symbolic value of Christian marriage. In Ephesians, Christian marriage is revealed to be a union imitating Christ's marriage to his church—an endless and eternal marriage.[15] After treating of the mutual relations between a husband and wife, Paul concludes by saying that marriage is actually a sign of Christ's union with his church. In other words, when a couple marry before the Christian community they are living signs revealing to the community God's love for all of us.[16]

The Marriage Act Is a Holy Act

Since Jesus' death is the perfect exemplar of all human acts of love, loving intercourse in marriage is also an act of total self-giving. Each spouse unreservedly gives himself or herself to the other. In that mutual self-giving, they image the self-giving of Jesus who died on the cross to give life. In the case of marriage, the self-giving of the spouses is ordered by the very nature of the marriage act to give birth to new life so that the child that is conceived is the completion of their mutual self-giving.[17] Their child—their image—is destined to live forever in holy union with the Father of us all.

And it is precisely here, in the realization of what could be, that childless couples through no fault of their own experience such pain (*CCC* 2374). They experience that somehow their love, no matter how great it is for one another, has not borne fruit in a child. Childless couples call forth the special compassion and understanding of the parish team.[18]

How mysterious are the ways of God! When one considers the number of couples who do not want children, who even abort children, why should a couple that wants their love to be completed in children be deprived of this greatest fruit? There is no human answer. Faith teaches us, however, that even without children, by their mutual self-giving, husband and wife realize their call to image God in his self-giving and thus realize themselves as persons.[19]

It should be noted that while not required by Christian love, the generosity of marital love can also be expressed through adoption. After all, the begetting of the child only begins the life of parenting. So even if the couples do not give natural birth to their children, a lifetime of devoted guiding, teaching, comforting and sharing with adopted children makes them true parents in every sense of the word. Realizing that there is more to parenting than birth, faith has moved many couples to adopt children. This act of generosity has provided a life of security and happiness for thousands of children who otherwise would be without the experience of parental love and the guidance of parental wisdom.

Spouses Imitate Jesus in the Marriage Act

In the most intimate act of the domestic church, couples give birth to children who, thanks to their parents' love, can obtain this eternal glory taught by our Catholic faith. Furthermore, in begetting their children, parents have the opportunity of reflecting Jesus' love for his Father as revealed in his moment of glory—his death on the cross—by their sacrifices. On the cross Jesus revealed his total submission to the will of the Father. In his death, Jesus gave all of himself perfectly and totally to the Father and to us. When Jesus died, he had absolutely nothing left to give. (After his death, with his resurrection, Jesus gave us his Spirit.[20])

At the Last Supper, Jesus revealed what total love is. During his final meal with them, he explained to the ones he loved so intensely the hidden dynamics that were actually at work in his crucifixion. It might seem to the apostles that evil had triumphed, but Jesus revealed that, in fact, he had won the decisive victory over all the forces of evil that so torment our world. Jesus' love had vanquished the devil and all his hateful works, and Jesus' victory allows all of us who believe in him to have eternal life.[21] It is no wonder that his last words on the cross before giving up his spirit to his Father are: "It is accomplished" (Jn 19:30). "I have perfectly accomplished your will; I did all you wanted done for eternal life."

The manner of Jesus' death was so holy, the Gospel of Mark records, that even pagans recognized Jesus' special relationship to God:

> The centurion who was standing opposite him, having seen how he died, said, "In truth this man was the Son of God" (Mk 15:39).

The fullness of the being of each spouse is communicated in the willingness to give life and not prevent it—as Jesus communicates life to us today by giving up his life on the cross. When stopping the transmission of life becomes the norm, communication is lessened, love dies, sex is frustrating, marriages are troubled, and the union may end in separation or divorce. Because contraception separates pleasure from the creative process, it separates pleasure from meaning and purpose and becomes simply an end in itself. Pleasure without purpose is ultimately frustrating to the human psyche. Most importantly, the couples do not grow in holiness.

On the other hand, in giving themselves to one another without prior restraint, the spouses also give themselves to God so that he might accomplish his will in their coming together, whatever his love thinks best: to beget life or not. So self-giving sexual love is a value in and of itself because it relates the spouses to God's love. It is not simply a means to procreation. Nevertheless, by its very nature, sexual love goes beyond itself to the begetting of new life.[22] The act of intercourse, then, requires the couples to trust the wisdom of God and his saving love, just as Jesus trusted himself to his Father when he gave himself up completely on the cross. In this way the couple and their family grow in holiness.

As couples who use natural methods of family planning attempt to grow in holiness, they experience a depth in their love. They seek natural practices of birth regulation, because nature itself—as ordered by Divine Wisdom—has periods when conception will not take place. It is perfectly in accord with the human intelligence to use this natural process to regulate births. In other words, it is not a teaching of the church that Catholics must have as many children as possible.[23]

This desire to utilize the natural periods of fecundity and infecundity to regulate births is an effect of grace and a gift from God (*CCC* 2368). It cannot be legislated or imposed. Rather, God gives the gift that allows couples to choose natural family planning with confidence, peace and serenity.[24]

Sexual pleasure is satisfying only when it is the expression and communication of the personal love of the spouses for one another in such a way that it is open to the possibility of a new creation. When we love, we want to create beauty: in an object or in a person. When we love a friend, we want to share with our friend our own beauty, which is why we cannot love others unless we first love ourselves. When parents love their children, they want to create beautiful children—moral, loving, integrated, and at peace.

In this creative act, of which child-bearing is only the beginning of the creation of another human being in the image and likeness of God through Christian child-rearing, the parents cooperate with the creative act of God himself.

> We [Christians] are God's masterpiece, created in Christ Jesus for good works as God intended from the beginning (Eph 2:10).

To Be Radically Open to the Transmission of Life Requires Trust

When couples trust God, he will enable them to be holy parents to the children they beget. Given the difficulties of raising children today, such dependent trust on the Father is not easy; for trust is never easy when great issues are at stake. Even Jesus had his agony in the garden; Luke says the experience was so devastating for Jesus that "an angel came to him from heaven to give him strength" (Lk 22:44).

When Jesus forbade divorce and his disciples said it was better not to marry, he responded: "It is not everyone who can accept this, but only those to whom it has been granted" (Mt 19:11). Again, when he said how difficult it is for the rich to enter the kingdom of God, and some of his listeners asked who, then, can be saved, Jesus responded: "Things that are impossible for men are possible for God" (Lk 18:27).

Grace Makes Trust Possible

In other words, although some couples find keeping every act of intercourse open to the transmission of holy life extremely difficult, they also find that grace makes it possible. As they grow in holiness, they experience for themselves what scripture reveals: grace works best when humans, in their weakness, turn to God their Father in loving trust.

When Paul asks for deliverance from his "thorn in the flesh" because it is so difficult to bear and he is so weak, Jesus responds, "My grace is enough for you: my power is at its best in weakness." Then Paul says:

> So I shall boast in my weaknesses so that the power of Christ may stay over me....For when I am weak, then I am strong (2 Cor 12:7-10).

The need for divine power in human weakness is affirmed again and again in the scriptures, and specifically in those areas of life we find especially difficult and challenging. The Jews called upon God to fight their battles against their enemies. The psalmists ask for God's power in meeting adversity, coping with life and growing in wisdom. Since sex is so powerful,[25] spouses can expect God's help in this area as well. The grace of God "puts both the will and the action" (Phil 2:13) into all of us who strive to live holy lives.

Rational planning of births in a family without resorting to immoral methods requires discipline, self-restraint and constant communication among the partners. These, in turn, increase the holiness of the couples in a way that blocking life transmission never can. The act of intercourse open to life requires complete trust in God, his wisdom, power and faithfulness, just as Jesus trusted his Father when he gave himself up on the cross. This, of course, is holiness, and holiness leads to praise.

> Glory be to him whose power, working in us, can do infinitely more than we can ask or imagine; glory be to him from generation to generation in the church and in Christ Jesus forever and ever. Amen (Eph 3:20-21).

Natural Family Planning Is Planning Families God's Way

Modern medical technology has provided couples with an intelligent way to control their fertility in marriage which is in harmony with their human, God-given nature and their dignity as persons made in his image. Providentially this has been discovered and perfected just at the time when contraception has been pushed by others who had no real concern about growing in holiness.

This method is called natural family planning.[26] It is "natural" because it is accomplished in harmony with natural processes of life-transmission. Natural family planning uses very reliable, scientific and proven-effective methods of determining female fertility periods which form the basis of spacing births. Natural family planning does not require taking unreasonable risks; yet, at the same time, it accepts fully God's gift of fertility.

> With a 99 percent effectiveness rate when the couple follows the rules, natural family planning (NFP) is potentially as effective as any method of family planning. The key to success lies in the hearts and minds of the couples who use it.[27]

Natural family planning receives support by active participation in the community of faith, both by the couple itself and by their offspring. Because of the openness of communication required by natural family planning, couples find themselves becoming more ready and willing to raise the children in holiness and to develop resources in terms of knowledge and the support of family and friends to raise them in a community that promotes holiness.

Finally, individual as well as community prayer is always necessary so that the strength of the angels may be imparted to God's human children as they turn to their Father in complete abandonment to his will. In fact, sociological studies reveal that when couples pray together daily, they significantly experience greater sexual fulfillment than those who do not.[28]

Because the sex urge is powerful, sexual attractions and relations are particularly difficult to relate to growth in holiness, especially in the beginning of acquiring virtue.[29] Yet, this too is part of the divine plan. God made sex powerful precisely because he knows well the difficulties involved in raising children. God wants to make our cooperation in his creation of new human persons a source of pleasure and joy, even though it is a hard task. "Be fruitful, multiply, fill the earth and conquer it" (Gen 1:28).

Children are a blessing from the Lord, and Christian married couples who seek union with God in holiness cannot let the wisdom of the world obscure their understanding and appreciation of their vocation: to communicate life, both human and divine, for now and for all eternity.

Life-Giving Human Sexuality Always Requires Self-Control[30]

Of course, as is obvious to all, it is hard to control sexual images, desires and activities. That is why Jesus cautions that discipline of the heart is the absolute first step to holy living. Jesus says:

> From the heart come evil desires: murder, adultery, fornication, theft, perjury, slander. These are the things that defile a person (Mt 15:18).

The act of adultery, for example, is first committed in the heart before it has expression in deed. Jesus says:

> If a man looks at a woman with lust, he has already committed adultery with her in his heart (Mt 5:27-28).[31]

In a lengthy section in the First Letter to the Corinthians, St. Paul gives the Christian faithful a divine perspective for the exercise of self-discipline in all matters, including sex: "The world as we know it is passing away" (1 Cor 7:29-31).[32]

Sex is holy because it communicates life. Therefore, it must always be exercised in a way that fosters life—now and for eternity. In spite of the difficulty which all human beings experience, sex cannot be allowed to run rampant. Sexual freedom is, in fact, not freedom. It is enslavement to the vicissitudes of passion and emotional turmoil and leads to great evils. Paul argues strenuously for bodily restraint in the Letter to the Colossians:

> You must put to death everything in you that belongs to earthly life: fornication, impurity, guilty passion, evil desires and greed, which is idolatry; all this makes God angry (Col 3:5).

The control both sex and even greed exercise over the human will is compared in many places in the scriptures to idolatry—the committed following of false gods. Lust and greed do not lead to union with the Father of our Lord Jesus Christ. They lead instead to a self-indulgence which ends up consuming those who are unrestrainedly greedy[33] and sexually active.

Celibacy and Virginity Accentuate the Holiness of Both Sex and Marriage

There is another tradition in the church which serves to accentuate the holiness with which the Bible and Christian tradition regard marriage and the use of sex within marriage— that is, the tradition of celibacy and virginity (*CCC* 1620).

The Lord did not command abstention from sex, as certain heresies in the past have taught.[34] Nevertheless, Paul thought that those who remained unmarried would be better able to devote themselves to the coming of the kingdom without the distraction of temporal affairs which are necessary to married life (cf. 1 Cor 7:32–43).[35]

The Catholic Church has institutionalized celibacy and virginity in the religious communities of men and women who vow themselves to poverty, chastity and obedience—the evangelical counsels, as they are called. Such vowed lives serve as an impressive counterpoint to the sanctity of marriage, for both vocations are for the good of the human race.

Marriage brings about the physical increase of the human race, and celibacy insofar as it is ordered to the contemplative life brings about its spiritual growth.[36]

This understanding of celibacy has become a part of the church's discipline with regard to priests in the Latin church. As Pope John Paul II explains:

> [Celibacy is] "a precious gift given by God to his church and as a sign of the kingdom which is not of this world — a sign of God's love for this world and of the undivided love of the priest for God and for God's people, with the result that celibacy is seen as a positive enrichment of the priesthood."[37]

The Chaste Single Is a Powerful Witness

Many Catholics today live chaste lives as single persons. Some have not yet married, some are widowed, some have suffered the pain of divorce, and some have simply never given themselves in marriage for a variety of reasons. Their chaste single lives also witness — indeed powerfully — to the sacredness of sex and the married life.

Given the state of our society today, these witnesses can seem out of step with reality, but then that has always been the case with Christians. We are counter-cultural, as the saying goes. That is, we do hold values that are opposed to the values of the world. Yet Christian values are better than the values of the world because they lead to peace and stability in family life on earth and to joy in eternal life. The challenge the parish team faces is to communicate this teaching of scripture and the church in a way that wins or attracts the assent of the faithful in parishes so that the parish can truly be in effect a "sign lifted up among the Gentiles."

The holiness of sexuality and chastity advocated by the church stands in stark contrast to the darkness of a neo-paganism which contemporary values promote in the area of sex. The Letter to the Ephesians gives a plan of action for the parish team when Paul describes the conditions of a world apart from the Lord and calls for a spiritual revolution so that Christians today may become ever more holy as they reflect the life of Christ in them to a world in darkness. We know, of course, that there are people who, for one reason or another, have not accepted the gospel—perhaps because they never had the opportunity to hear it. Nevertheless, they lead good lives and try to be examples of decency and justice to their families and to others. Only God in his infinite mercy and wisdom is able to judge them.[38] Paul is not writing about them.

Paul's pagans are those whose goal is personal satisfaction and pleasure, no matter what pain their way of life may cause others. They are intellectually in the dark, and they are strangers to a way of life lived in union with God. Furthermore, Paul says that because they have refused to listen to God, they are no longer sensitive to issues of what is right or wrong. Instead, they have given in totally to being estranged from the life of God, without knowledge of right or wrong, because they have shut their hearts to it. In fact, they willingly pursue sexual pleasure and indecency of every kind. As for the Christian person of faith, Paul says: "Your mind must be renewed so that you can put on the new self that has been created in God's way, in the goodness and holiness of the truth" (Eph 4:17–24).

Human beings are both called and empowered to reflect the radiance of Christ himself in all their actions. We have been delivered from the power of darkness and been given all the graces we need to act in a manner consistent with the gospel. United to Christ, our good shepherd, we will be able to enjoy the fruits of the Spirit and share our own joy and holiness with all those the Lord puts in our path.

The Preaching of the Gospel Is a Vocation of Glory

All that we have said in this book shows us that the vocation of the Catholic preacher, educator, and parent is a call to spread the glory of God. When Paul describes his own ministry, he describes our contemporary ministry as well:

> We are ministers of a new covenant, not of written letters but of the Spirit; the written letter kills, but the Spirit gives life (2 Cor 3:4–6).

7

Holiness Results in a Holy Life-Style

*C*hapter One described some of the significant cultural changes that affect the living out of the Catholic faith in today's world. The most basic change is the perception that religion and morality are totally a matter of private judgment.[1] When carried to extremes by the influence of secular humanism, there results a mistaken notion that there is no objective, universal truth, including the revealed truths of faith and, as a consequence, no universal moral law binding on all persons. In *Fides et Ratio (Faith and Reason)*, Pope John Paul II wrote:

> There is a tendency to grant to the individual conscience the prerogative of independently determining the criteria of good and evil and then acting accordingly. Such an outlook is quite congenial to an individualistic ethic, wherein each individual is faced with his own truth different from the truth of others (n. 98).[2]

Because religion no longer seems to offer clear and assured knowledge about the most basic and most essential truths and values of human existence, as the Second Vatican Council put it, "Growing numbers of people are abandoning religion in practice."[3] In the light of this falling away from religious practice, it becomes ever more vital that the entire parish team focus on showing that the holiness we have been exploring is God's gift that makes the joy of the gospel real in the lives of the faithful. The joy of holiness is the good news of salvation. The greatest tool the team has in bringing their fellow parishioners to the joy of gospel living is the gospel itself as passed on through the church. Pope John Paul II recognizes the need of newly invigorated gospel proclamation when he writes:

> There is today no more urgent preparation [for the defense of human dignity and the proclamation of the gospel message] than this: to lead people to discover both their capacity to know the truth and their yearning for the ultimate and definitive meaning of life.[4]

The parish team with its diversely gifted members is the key agent of renewal at the level where the church most intimately interacts with the faithful who still look to the church for both moral guidance and spiritual nourishment. Through their ministry, the lay members of the team, parents, teachers, and ministers, have a privileged responsibility to build up the body of Christ in this cultural crisis. With a renewed parish and its programs of outreach the larger society will also be touched and strengthened by gospel power.

> The church is fully aware of a pastoral urgency that calls for an absolutely special concern for culture in those circumstances where the development of culture becomes disassociated not only from the Christian faith but even from human values....The church calls upon the lay faithful to be present, as signs of courage and intellectual creativity, in the privileged places of culture [education, scientific research, artistic creativity, work in the humanities].[5]

Although there are flaws and difficulties in contemporary culture, technology and science have without doubt improved the quality of human life in all regions of the world whose political and economic situation allows them to utilize these resources. Again, John Paul II puts culture into perspective:

This heightened sense of the dignity of the human person and of his or her uniqueness, and of the respect due to the journey of conscience, certainly represents one of the positive achievements of modern culture.[6]

Catholics Have Been Greatly Blessed by the American Culture

The most obvious blessing is that Catholics have gotten richer. Sons and daughters of poor immigrants, or perhaps grandchildren of poor immigrants, American Catholics have climbed the economic ladder. Thirty percent earned more than $30,000 per year in 1985.[7] They own their own homes, have their own automobiles, hold responsible positions in business.[8] Their children are becoming well-educated, even at more prestigious schools. Seventeen percent are college graduates.[9] Since 29% of Catholics are under thirty years of age and 36% between thirty and forty-nine,[10] continued upward movement seems likely as their children grow up.

Such economic progress, of course, is a true blessing from a loving Father. Everyone should have enough money to be free from a daily struggle for survival. While poverty is looked upon positively as a virtue in the Christian tradition, destitution is not.

In spite of these successes, however, there still remain a large number of Catholics who do not enjoy the shared economic benefits formerly reserved for the rich alone.[11] But even these "poor" are enjoying a higher standard of living than their forebears and, more to the point, are absorbing the economic values of the upwardly mobile.[12]

Unfortunately, there is also a down side to the new wealth of Catholics. The greater wealth, and the life-styles this wealth enables individuals and families to pursue,[13] have contributed greatly to the decline in the sense of the holy in life, evidenced by how they regard moral issues. In 1969, 72% of the Catholic population thought premarital sex was "wrong."

In 1985, only 33% thought it was "wrong," while 58% had no moral objection to it. This is at variance with other Christian denominations. While approval of premarital sex increased among all denominations, Catholics were the most permissive; 48% of Protestants still disapproved, and only 46% approved. The writers explain this discrepancy by saying that "the birth control issue has damaged the church's credibility on other sex-related issues."[14] However valid this explanation of their statistics is, it is not the only possible explanation of change in moral viewpoint.

Material prosperity and the energy it takes to maintain it in a highly competitive world make it difficult for most Catholics to be awed by the presence of the holy in their lives or to maintain a sense of God's presence in all that they do.

Given the competitive nature of business, it would not be at all surprising to learn that many wealthy people have cut corners when it comes to honesty in business transactions. Indeed, newspapers are filled with accounts of frauds, insider deals, misappropriation and embezzlements. These are all forms of evil to which the love of money leads. And with it, of course, is the loss of the sense of the holy.

Love of money radically changes our life-style, because greed clouds our sense of right and wrong and blinds us to the nature of love. An excellent example of this loss of values is found in a single verse of John's Gospel. The scene is a dinner in Bethany where Mary, sister of Lazarus, anoints the feet of Jesus with very expensive ointment. Judas Iscariot complains of the waste of expensive ointment because he did not recognize the love of Jesus which it indicated, nor did he appreciate the mystery of redemption which it foreshadowed. Scripture comments on Judas' complaint:

> He said this, not because the poor mattered to him, but because he was a thief; he was in charge of the common purse and used to steal from it (Jn 12:6).

So parish team members have a challenging ministry: to restore in parish life a sense of the holy in dealing with money.[15]

Jesus Loves the Poor

There is a very touching scene recorded by Mark when Jesus observed a poor widow put two small coins worth practically nothing into the temple treasury. He pointed her out to his disciples and said:

> Amen, I say to you, this poor widow put in more than all the others. For they all gave from their abundance, but she, from her poverty, has contributed all she had, her whole livelihood (Mk 12:42-44).

The rich can buy good education, provide for their own needs, and determine the course of their lives. The poor, on the other hand, like the poor widow, have no alternative but to trust in God's providence. It seems easier for the poor to respond instantaneously to the interior movements of the Spirit because they have nothing to lose and everything to gain. The rich, on the other hand, have so much that they cannot give up their wealth for gospel priorities.

One time a rich aristocrat was told by Jesus how he could inherit eternal life:

> Sell all that you own and distribute the money to the poor, and you will have treasure in heaven; then come, follow me.

The rich man went away "filled with sadness, for he was very rich" (Lk 18:24-27).

Scripture Gives Hope to the Poor

The Gospel of Matthew presents Jesus as the great prophet of the new covenant; he is the new Moses. So Jesus goes to the mountain top where he begins to proclaim to the crowds the nature of the kingdom of heaven he is establishing on earth. Whereas God spoke to Moses in the midst of thunder and flame, Jesus begins quietly to speak a series of blessings filled with hope for the future. The first manifestation of God to Moses was fearsome; Jesus' words to us are awesome as he reveals the spirit of the new covenant, the covenant ratified not by the blood of goats and bulls, but by Jesus' own blood on the cross. The very first beatitude in the first gospel, that of Matthew, describes the kingdom of heaven as belonging to the poor.

> Blessed are the poor in spirit,
>   theirs is the kingdom of heaven (Mt 5:3).

Poverty is also paramount in the Gospel of Luke. In the twelfth chapter, Jesus gives a lengthy teaching on the importance of poverty for freeing his followers to put their trust totally in the Father. The Father knows, Jesus says, that we need clothes to wear and things to eat and drink, and the Father will provide us with all these things as we need them. With confidence in the Father's care, therefore, we are free to devote our energies to working on behalf of the kingdom of God; in short, we are free to pursue holiness as our vocation in life. We will never lack for the necessities of life (Lk 12:29–32).

The Gospel of Luke, in fact, goes further than Matthew with regard to Christian poverty. Instead of extolling those who are "poor in spirit," which could mean even the wealthy who are detached from their wealth,[16] Luke teaches that the kingdom of God is for the physically poor.[17] In fact, Luke adds that those who are rich are getting their consolation now to such an extent that they cannot look forward to a heavenly reward (cf. Lk 6:24).

Luke recounts Jesus' parable about a poor man, Lazarus, who goes to heaven, while the rich man at whose gate Lazarus lay begging went to Hades. The rich man's offense, it seems from the parable, was his great wealth (cf. Lk 16:19–31).

For Luke, money is so attractive that it can enslave; therefore his gospel sets the standard for poverty as being actual poverty (not destitution, of course) and not just detachment from material goods as in Matthew. He quotes Jesus:

> No servant can be the slave of two masters....You cannot be the slave of both God and money (Lk 16:13).

Paul amplifies the contemporary relevance of Jesus' teaching when he writes, "The love of money is the root of all evil" (1 Tim 6:9-10). The reason is that greed twists our values; it makes us go after things we would be better off without, even if it means abandoning faith and the pursuit of virtue, even if it means doing harm to others. Ultimately such a pursuit will destroy the seeker.

The Parish Team Needs To Preach about Money

In the eucharistic liturgy, the Catholic community gives thanks to the Father for all his gifts to us. Mass celebrates the mysterious holiness of God manifested in his creative acts and his providential generosity. It is important, therefore, for the parish team to preach about God's gifts to his people. There is, of course, no need to give thanks if we provide for ourselves, which the rich think they do. Since the rich are surrounded by the work of their own hands, they do not see the world as the work of a creator who is worthy of praise. Awe for the generosity of the giver of gifts and creator of the universe is essential to worship, whereas the love of money distorts human vision and obscures the holiness of God. Praise comes from grateful and humble hearts, after all.

The task, then, of parish team members today is to prepare their people for divine worship in the Mass and the sacraments by showing them the connection between God's activity in their daily lives and the liturgy of the church. Parish team members need to communicate the gospel in such a way that Catholics become more attuned to the gospel teachings regarding holiness and more sensitive to life-styles that impede growth in holiness. This begins with giving teachings on the most basic element of all life-styles: money.

Scripture Does Not Require Destitution for Holiness

St. Paul in his Second Letter to the Corinthians sets out some principles regarding the use of money which are very helpful to Catholics who seriously wish to grow in holiness, yet at the same time must earn sufficient income to provide for the needs of their families in a very expensive American society.

When he was taking up a collection for distribution to the poor in the church of Jerusalem, Paul urged the Corinthians to be generous, but at the same time he recognized the practical problems that giving away money entails. Paul did not expect them to deny themselves the usual amenities of life, nor did he indicate that they should make life difficult for themselves and their families. What Paul teaches is that the Christian should always be prepared to help the needy from his or her surplus. At the same time, the recipient of another's generosity should always be prepared to return the favor when he or she can. "That is how we strike a balance" (2 Cor 8:12-15).

In the same letter, under the inspiration of the Holy Spirit, Paul reaffirms the promise of Jesus that the almsgiver will always be repaid. Not only will God provide all that we need, he will increase our contributions and make them even bigger fruit than we could have imagined. For our generosity, God will be praised by the less fortunate—surely a blessing in which we should rejoice (2 Cor 9: 10-11).

Changes in Married Life Affect
How Catholics Esteem Children

A second great cultural change that affects Catholic parents in particular is the way our culture views children.

God intends that men and women marry for life and have children, thereby creating with God himself citizens of the heavenly kingdom.[18] The holy married couple therefore regard their union as a way to holiness and look upon their children as a blessing.

Two factors are seriously distorting this Christian teaching. First, the frequency and social acceptability of divorce are causing instability in family life today even among Catholics. In 1985, ten percent of Catholics were divorced or separated, doubling from 1976. Furthermore, one out of every four Catholic teenagers said their parents have divorced—an astounding figure, which is the same rate found in the general population.[19] For many, marriage is not a lifetime union, but there is growing scientific evidence that children cannot be properly formed in a temporary and sometimes hostile environment. Secondly, secular society regards children more as a burden than a blessing, since they have become an economic liability. It costs a great deal to give birth, to feed, clothe, and provide health care, and above all to educate a child. In former ages, children were welcomed because they were more hands to work for the family's well-being. While in other cultures this is still true, in the United States children do not contribute to a family's resources; rather they drain them. And this is affecting the way large numbers of Catholics view having children.

In 1968, fifty percent of Catholics thought four children was the ideal number; in 1985, only nine percent chose to have four or more.[20] This is a huge drop of 41% in only seventeen years, indicating a major revision of family values in general, and of values regarding children in particular.

Because the birthing, nurturing and education of children are no longer the main priority of large numbers of families, extensive services of the church in this area are no longer required. Catholic schools, for example, are closing all over the country, and the trend is unlikely to be reversed in the foreseeable future. In 1969 there were 1,334 Catholic high schools and 10,050 Catholic elementary schools, serving a Catholic population of 47,873,238. In 1998 there were 790 Catholic high schools and 6,818 Catholic elementary schools, serving a Catholic population of 61,567,769.[21]

The education of youth was once a significant focus of the ministry of priests and religious women. Priests were role-models for young boys, women religious for young girls. Today, few priests devote much time to the difficult and demanding ministry of working with young people.[22] More significantly, perhaps, the education of children is no longer a vocational goal of women religious. Nevertheless, youth is still a major concern of parishes; yet instead of being able to use priests and religious, more and more parishes employ lay teachers in their schools and special youth ministers to provide programs for adolescents. So long as the baptized faithful are employed by the church, it is still the church who ministers to youth through the exercise of the gifts of the Spirit given at baptism and strengthened at confirmation.

The Parish Needs To Re-Establish the Value of Children

To reverse this massive change in attitude, those who constitute the parish team need to explain and witness to the incomparable value of children as revealed in the holy scriptures and taught by the church. Secularization of culture has had such a profound impact that the reversal will be extremely difficult.

The first step in that reversal, however, is for all Catholics—family members and ministers of the gospel—to see children as God's greatest blessing to married couples. This is what scripture reveals. This does not mean that every couple must have as many children as possible, but it does mean that holy people who seek to grow in holiness will regard the children born to them with respect and love as blessings from God.[23] Scripture exalts the place of children in human life. The psalmist says:

> Sons are a gift from the Lord;
>> the fruit of the womb is a reward.
> Like the arrows in the hand of a warrior
>> are the sons you father when young (Ps 127:3-4).[24]

This cannot be reduced to mere cultural influence in a day when sons were an economic necessity. Bearing children was considered the greatest work of women, and the Old Testament is filled with examples of women longing to be fruitful. The story of Hannah's barrenness begins the First Book of Samuel, and her song of thanksgiving for the birth of Samuel (cf. 1 Sam 1:1-2:11) is the basis for Mary's Magnificat in the Gospel of Luke (cf. Lk 1:46-55).

The psalmist reflects on the goodness of God when he sings:

> He enthrones the barren woman in her house
>> by making her the happy mother of sons (Ps 113:9).

And the Book of Proverbs says:

> The crown of the aged is their children's children (Prov 17:6).

God has ordained that human parents be instruments by which he populates his heavenly courts. Therefore the very act of intercourse is holy because it leads to begetting holy people and to glorifying God. Nature itself substantiates the incomparable value of new human life since it has made it so difficult for such life to be aborted. In times past, before abortion became a practical alternative, parents killed infants already born. This was one of the great crimes against the people of God which motivated God to send the savior, Moses, to deliver them from the hand of Pharaoh. In the speech that precipitated his death, Stephen said to the Jews:

> [Pharaoh] took advantage of our race, and mistreated our ancestors, forcing them to expose their babies to prevent their surviving (Acts 7:19).

Parents Prepare Their Children for Heavenly Glory

Since children who are conceived will live forever, God, in his great mercy, has destined them in and through Jesus Christ for union with him in his heavenly kingdom. Nonetheless, because they are free, thinking beings, children must be prepared for this glorious destiny.

This means that the parents' vocation, under the guidance of and in collaboration with the church and its ministers, is primarily one of raising children fit to enter the kingdom of heaven. Parents are the living scriptures for their children because they reveal God's infinite love for them and give them the assurance of God's continuing protection throughout their lives.[25] Jesus himself speaks to the education of children when he tells his disciples that to welcome a little child is to welcome Jesus himself. And one who does anything that draws the child away from faith in Jesus "would be better drowned in the depth of the sea with a great millstone around his neck" (Mt 18:5-6).

The Old Testament had already emphasized the importance of passing faith on to the children. The Book of Deuteronomy stresses the importance of knowing God's word, and also of making sure that knowledge of his word was passed on to the young. So important was the word of God that devout Israelites would actually bind small scrolls of scripture on the hands and around their head. The custom continues among the Orthodox Jews even to this day. Deuteronomy also called for a small plaque containing scripture to be attached to the entrance to the house of the devout. These evidences of devotion to God's law would be powerful signs to the young Israelite to follow in the way of his fathers (Dt 11:18-21).

Psalm 78 says that God "gave our ancestors strict orders to teach the law to their children," so that their children would be able to put their confidence in God because they would remember God's mighty deeds. (Ps 78:5-7)

In fact, so important is it for children to be formed in the word of God and to live by faith that Ben Sirach says that if children do not have a fear and reverence for the Lord, they will not have a long life (a biblical image for a successful life). In fact, Ben Sirach says it is better to have only one child who loves God than to have many children who are sinners. It is "better to die childless than have godless ones" (Sir 16:1-4).

The most beautiful praise of children is found in Psalm 128, which sings of the special praises of God to the devout. While the psalm is phrased in the language and customs of the society for which it was written, it was preserved in the canon of inspired literature because God wanted Christians not only yesterday but today and tomorrow to recognize his blessings in family life:

> Happy, all those who fear the Lord
> and walk in his ways.
> You will eat what your hands have worked for;
> happiness and prosperity will be yours.
> Your children will be around your table
> like shoots around an olive tree.
> Thus is the one blessed
> who fears the Lord (Ps 128:2-4).

The Parish Team Leads People
in the Ways of Holiness

Jesus said: "I have come that they may have life and have it more abundantly" (Jn 10:10). The whole purpose of the divine plan of creation is to make people who will be united in holiness with the God of holiness forever. Our union with him depends upon and results in our participation in the divine holiness whereby we give glory to God.

Today, in spite of the great difficulties the parish team faces in communicating the divine law in a secularistic culture, its members have a remarkable opportunity to lead their people into the ways of holiness. John Paul II said: "What is needed is to *first remake the Christian fabric of the ecclesial community itself* present...."[26] People of good will are hungry today for guidance; they want to do what is right for themselves and their children, but all too often they do not know the proper path to follow. The parish team can point out the way in a gentle and loving manner.

If law is imposed upon people in an authoritarian manner, without adequately respecting their personal freedom, they will not listen and, therefore, will not know the way of salvation. God has given each Catholic a sacred vocation to be one of God's children. The expression of the common vocation varies: marriage, celibacy, religious life, priesthood, single life. Common to all these vocations, however, is the call to be holy in the vocation. This call to holiness is answered through the movements of the Holy Spirit in the life of each (cf. Rom 8), so when the parish team proclaims the moral requirements of the Gospel of Jesus Christ as good news, giving new life to those who believe, the believers will respond, follow, and be healed.

For this reason, the Second Vatican Council speaks to priests, but its words apply equally to all who communicate the gospel message in the name of the church:

As educators in the faith, priests must see to it, either by themselves or through others, that the faithful are led individually in the Holy Spirit to a development of their own vocation as required by the gospel, to a sincere and active charity, and to that freedom with which Christ has made us free.[27]

8

Holiness Leads to Social Justice

*I*n the previous chapters we saw that the parish formation team is concerned with revealing how God's law guides the deepest movements of the human heart and thereby develops and enriches it. In this chapter we will explore how, through ordering the human heart toward being a just and fair person, the parish team sets the members of the parish firmly on the path to holiness and eternal glory. In spite of the intricacies of contemporary law and the maze of sometimes intense disputes about complex social justice issues, the team can, by understanding and preaching on the virtue of justice, lead the parish on the gospel way to holiness.

All Christians, but especially parish team leaders, have a grave obligation to be familiar with the basic principles and issues pertaining to justice and to act justly in the matters affecting them personally. The virtue of justice is the bedrock of Christian life in terms of our relations to all our fellow human beings, whether they are believers or not. Justice is an equation of equality between moral persons, either individuals or organizations.[1] It is concerned with basic fairness in human relationships.[2] Today this means that individual Catholics as well as Catholic parishes need to be especially sensitive to problems and questions of social justice.[3]

The Virtue of Justice Is Essential to Being Holy

St. Thomas Aquinas defines the virtue of justice as a habit whereby one person by a constant and perpetual will gives to another person what is the other's due.[4] That is, the just person always and perseveringly gives to everyone his or her right: what is owed to each, whether the other has a right to goods, honor or service.[5] Justice makes Christians holy by giving them the power willingly to render to others the duty they owe them whether or not the other is also a believer.[6]

Justice, therefore, as an attitude and habit of the heart, enables us to appreciate the wonderful diversity of God's gifts among human beings by giving us ease and delight in respecting and honoring the rights of others. God has given each person certain gifts and talents for the betterment of the whole human society,[7] but we cannot exercise those gifts unless we are inwardly free to do so. The virtue of justice gives us that freedom so we can give all persons the right to exercise their divine gifts in accord with the divine will. Justice, then, allows and promotes true human freedom; and justice, when lived by individuals, results in just communities and societies.

For example, in a family each child is different; parents cannot make all their children act the same or think the same way—nor should they want to—but when they treat each child in accord with the child's gifts, appreciating the uniqueness of each, the child flourishes and the family is enriched by the talents of each member. So in society, justice allows each unique person to be free to contribute his or her gifts to the welfare of all.

Thus, the parish team leaders begin to form the people of God in justice by leading them to appreciate the gifts God has given to all the people he has created, whether they are believers or not. God's gifts to them are the basis for their rights. When seen in this way, giving others the justice that is due them is not a burden but a joy. In being just, believers are being holy and, therefore, they also possess the joy of holiness.

Sources of Rights and Kinds of Justice

Each human right is a gift from God[8] and derives from one of three sources: (1) nature itself (i.e., a natural right, such as the right to basic food and drink); (2) private agreement (e.g., a contract, such as an agreement to work for a certain wage); or (3) positive law (i.e., a legal right arising from legislative, judicial or executive action). Whenever a right arises from one of these sources, justice imposes a corresponding duty in others to respect that right. Each of these kinds of rights also gives rise to special circumstances which must be taken into account when determining what is just.[9]

Justice is divided into three kinds: (1) *Legal justice* relates individuals to the good of their communities. This requires obedience to the laws of society and the rendering of service to society, such as military service or jury duty. (2) *Commutative justice* (taken from the Latin word *comuto*, meaning exchange or barter) establishes and maintains an equation of equality between persons in matters between them, such as in buying and selling properties and working for wages. (3) *Distributive justice* regulates society's distribution of its resources for the common good of all—how water is distributed equitably, for example, or how the environment is protected.[10]

Social Justice

Contemporary discussion of justice is deeply concerned with *social justice*. This is not a distinct kind of justice, but a phrase indicative of a multi-dimensional consideration of an issue, or issues, involving one or more of the three types of justice, and existing within the context of a particular human situation or interaction. All justice is social justice in the sense that it moderates relations with other people and therefore regulates society, both individually and corporately, as we have seen. But the term *social justice* is used to stress those aspects of particular cases that affect more than one individual in dealing with another. The term embraces the entire dynamic system of justice: legal justice, commutative justice and distributive justice. It also includes the consequences of any injustices in these areas in terms of the harm done to society as a whole or particular groups within society.[11]

Social justice in the modern world is a fluid concept; thus, without a stable point of reference, it is prone to the fatal flaw of relativism so prevalent in society as a whole today. However, *social justice* as taught by the Catholic Church, while still a fluid and dynamic concept, is firmly grounded in both natural law and the gospel of Jesus Christ.

At the center of all the church's concern for social justice is the individual person, made in the image and likeness of God and destined to be united with him forever. As Paul put it so eloquently and with such passion:

> Before the world was made, God chose us in Christ to be holy and spotless and to live through love in his presence, determining that we should become his adopted children through Jesus Christ (Eph 1:4-5).

For this reason, no matter how far-reaching the ramifications of economic issues may extend in terms of nations and the international community, the church is ultimately concerned with the betterment of each individual so that each may grow in holiness and be united as one in the body of Christ (Eph 4:15-16).

Justice Deals with Complex Issues

No one person can be an expert in legal, commutative and distributive justice and the myriad of issues that justice must deal with. Lawyers devote years of their life to becoming expert in one small field of law: tax lawyers, patent attorneys, trial lawyers, and the like. Consensus among those concerned with justice issues, even among the "experts," is usually reached only with difficulty and often involves compromise.

The National Conference of Catholic Bishops and their efforts to deal with social justice questions raised by American foreign policy in Vietnam and South America, and particular problems of economic justice and racism in the United States, are good examples of the difficulties of both arriving at consistent principles and communicating those principles to the American public with a single voice of authority that will have an influence on public national policy.[12] For example, the bishops, when they were drafting their pastoral letters on the economy and war and peace, called in many experts to consult with them in the formulation of their final documents, and even after their promulgation other experts contested their findings.[13]

Consequently, it is unreasonable to expect that priests, deacons, domestic missionaries, religion teachers, parents and other parish leaders will be able to preach as experts on the specific issues or aspects of social justice. They can, however, be expected to preach authoritatively—and with gospel power and insight—on the virtue of justice and its essential relationship to Christ's revelation and death on the cross. Leaders of the faith must be expected to instill and foster in those to whom they minister a deep appreciation and understanding that true social justice is predicated on one's personal relationship with Christ both as a member of Christ's Church and as one in whom the Holy Trinity has made its dwelling place.[14] Society consists of individuals in relationship to one another; social justice results when such relationships are extensions of individual lives based on gospel truth. Since the virtue of justice is what makes persons just, only just persons can make their society just.[15]

Christians Add Love and Mercy to Justice

As essential as justice is, justice alone is not enough for the person of faith to achieve the holiness of the gospel. The person seeking to be holy must add love to justice because love is the key that opens the gates of heaven and provides the basis for a life of joy and peace on earth.

In *Dives in Misericordia (Rich in Mercy),* Pope John Paul II wrote:

> Justice alone is not enough; it can even lead to the negation and destruction of itself, if that deeper power which is love is not allowed to shape human life in its various dimensions.[16]

In this moving encyclical, the pope recounts the story of the prodigal son (Lk 15: 40-54) in which the father goes far beyond justice when he restores his son to his full status as son. He goes even further when he shows his joy at the son's restoration by throwing a party for him to celebrate his return. In this case, "Love is transformed into mercy when it is necessary to go beyond the precise norm of justice—precise and often too narrow."[17]

Mercy goes still further; not only does it forgive offenses and injustices, it restores the offender to the place of honor that had been lost by the offense.[18]

While love with its accompanying mercy, which is at the very heart of the mystery of Christ, goes beyond justice, it nevertheless presupposes and builds on justice. Without justice, there can be no real love, because at the basis of love is the desire for the full good of the other, which includes the full respect of all the natural rights belonging to the human person. In other words, you cannot really love other persons if at the same time you deny them what you owe them in justice.[19]

Catholic Moral Teaching Rests on Justice and Merciful Love

Justice and love are the virtues on which rest all of Catholic moral teaching governing social relations in terms of external human actions. When the parish team communicates the gospel teaching on justice as brought to perfection by love and mercy, they are contributing to the full development of all human society since their hearers are God's instruments by which God extends his mercy to the entire world. By giving witness to the truth, Catholics share with others the mystery of the heavenly Father's love. As a consequence, people throughout the world will be aroused to a lively hope— the gift of the Holy Spirit—so that they will finally be caught up in the peace and utter happiness of that land radiant with the splendor of the Lord.[20]

Human Justice Participates in God's Own Justice

Scripture affirms that all just human laws partake to varying degrees in the wisdom and, therefore, the holiness of God. The Book of Sirach says: "All wisdom is from the Lord, and it is his own forever" (Sir 1:1).

In his Second Letter to the Corinthians, Paul explains that to know God and follow his commands is to share in God's glory, which, in fact, is the same glory which shines now on the face of the exalted Christ. Therefore, to follow God's commands is to tread the path to holiness (cf. 2 Cor 4:6). Furthermore, in bestowing the gift of his son upon us,

God established for Christians a new norm of justice—one which supersedes and puts into perspective all previous efforts to be just. For Jesus himself becomes the norm of justice, a justice tempered always by mercy; it is a justice alive with the life of Christ animating all those who are just and actively seek after justice for all (cf. Gal 2:20-21).

In the teaching of Jesus[21] we have the basis for how contemporary Christians can make valid judgments regarding human laws that will enable them to partake more fully in the wisdom of God, share in the glory of his providential governance and grow in holiness.

Consequently, the whole mission of the church carried on by the parish team leaders is to fill the faithful with a sense of God's own justice. God's justice is made visible in Christ, and by imitating Jesus, the believer becomes perfect as our heavenly Father is perfect—perfect in all things, including the willingness to render to each what is his or her due.[22] As Pope John Paul II says:

> The redemption of the world—this tremendous mystery of love in which creation is renewed—is, at its deepest root, the fullness of justice in a human heart—the heart of the first-born Son.

Sacred Scripture Teaches Us That Just Governance Is a Gift from God

When God led the Israelites out of Egypt, he took them to Mount Sinai, and there in a terrifying display of divine power and glory he gave them laws to live by. To the laws he attached a promise: if they would live according to the laws he was giving them, they would be God's own people and he would give them a land for their own. When Moses came down from the mountain, his face reflected the glory of the Most High so brightly that the people could not look at him (Ex 24:12-16).[24]

Ever since that awe-inspiring revelation to Moses on Mount Sinai, the Jews have been the people of the Law, God's own most sacred Law. Psalm 119 is a long poem in praise of God's law:

> How happy those of blameless life
>> who walk in the Law of the Lord God (Ps 119:1).

The Book of Proverbs attributes all human power to govern people and make laws ultimately to the wisdom of God and his eternal Law. For Wisdom says:

> By me monarchs rule and princes issue just laws;
>> by me rulers govern,
>> and the great impose justice on the world (Prov 8:15-16).

When the Pharisees tried to get Jesus to speak against Roman authority so that they could persuade the Roman governor to stop his preaching, they asked Jesus about the Jews' responsibility to obey Roman law. Did Jews have to support the foreign state? Did they have to pay taxes? In response, taking the tax coin Jesus said only: "Give back to Caesar what is Caesar's, and to God what belongs to God."[25] This vague statement by which Jesus avoided the trap they had set for him has been variously interpreted throughout the centuries, each epoch seeing in it justification for their own attitudes toward the government. In the context of the exchange with the Pharisees, Jesus acknowledges the right of society to pass laws demanding the payment of taxes. At the same time, he affirms that God must also be given what is due him.

On trial before Pontius Pilate, who ultimately condemned Jesus to crucifixion, Jesus revealed the divine origin of all worldly power. At first Jesus refused to answer Pilate's question about his origin, and Pilate rebuked him, saying: "Surely you know I have power to release you and I have power to crucify you?" To this Jesus replied simply: "You would have no power over me if it had not been given you from above,"[26] acknowledging that the human power of governance comes from God and not from the state.

In the United States, a democracy, the power of governance still ultimately comes from God, but through the mediation of the voters who elect those who are given the task of governing them. As a result, one could call the voters the real rulers of the country. So the power does indeed come from the consent of the governed, but only because God works through democracy as much as when he works through monarchy.[27]

In the Letter to the Romans, St. Paul develops Jesus' understanding of the source of the power. All power comes from God; even the civil authorities are appointed by God. Therefore, the Christian citizens are required to obey the governing authorities; to resist their authority is in fact resisting God's plan of governance, and those who do so will be punished for the offense. Paul notes that good behavior is not afraid of magistrates; only criminals have anything to fear. Therefore, to avoid being afraid, live honestly, and indeed you may even be honored by the civic authorities.

Paul is convinced that the state is an instrument of God for the well-being of the citizenry and that the power to punish is an important part of the proper exercise of authority. Hence, the Christian owes obedience to the state, including paying taxes. He says: "Pay every government official what he has a right to ask—whether it be direct tax or indirect, fear or honor" (cf. Rom 13:1-7).

Now, of course, in this passage Paul is not dealing with the serious conflicts that arise when society enforces unjust laws or when dictators hold their people in tyrannical bondage. He is not concerned with the morality of a just revolution against a tyrannical ruling power, nor with the resolution of tribal and ethnic conflicts for supremacy, such as the world is seeing unfold in Africa, the Middle East and the Balkans. Rather, Paul is assuming that the laws are just and intended for the good of the people they govern. Ultimately, he says, such laws come from God.[28]

So that Christians might live under just laws and leaders, Paul urges Christians to pray for their leaders. In the general intercessions at Mass, Catholics pray not only for church leaders, but also for all civic leaders. This is particularly important in a democracy where the officials are elected by the people and are responsible to them for the welfare of the country and states. We pray that they will govern well so that we may live in peace and quiet and worship God (1 Tim 2:1-2).

God Judges Justly

Various passages in scripture, particularly in the Old Testament, praise God for judging all rightly and with mercy. God punishes evil and rewards the holy one by listening to their cries for help (Ps 34:11, 16-18). Since God's laws reflect his own wisdom, those who obey God's laws and follow his teachings share in the wisdom of God himself. One could say that the obedient are wise like God (cf. Ps 119).

Once again, this teaching of scripture demonstrates how important the ministry of the parish team is. Through its proclamation of God's word, the team extends God's wisdom into the life of the parish and all its members. A wise community is a community of both peace and justice.

Adam and Eve's Sin Against Justice Brought About the Fullness of Justice

The story of Adam and Eve is the story of primal injustice.[29] By knowingly and willingly violating God's positive and expressed command, Adam and Eve sinned against justice: they violated God's right to their obedience as his creatures; obedience was the just return for all the gifts God bestowed on them.[30] They disobeyed with deliberate malice, without the influence of passion or the weakness of our fallen nature; they disobeyed knowing it was terribly wrong, yet their prideful will to be equal to God moved them to sin. The enormity of their malicious injustice is attested to by the enormity[31] of their punishment which was passed on to all their descendants: women would bear children in pain, and men would have pain in their work.[32] And, finally, they were expelled from the garden of happiness and the tree of life.

God in his infinite mercy, however, decided to reestablish the fullness of justice through his merciful sending of his only-begotten Son to redeem the world from all injustice. The price of our redemption and the possibility of peace and justice on earth and eternal life in heaven was nothing less than Jesus' own blood, shed on the cross of Calvary (1 Pet 1:18–19).

Jesus Brings God's Law to Perfection

Jesus brings the Law first revealed to Moses to fulfillment. In doing so, however, he requires that his followers go beyond the mere observances of the Mosaic Law itself to the deepest movements of the heart which the Law is intended to direct and from which all our human actions flow.[33]

The Gospel of Matthew considers this new orientation of Jesus' teaching extensively in Chapter 15:1-20. Stressing that mere ritual observance of the law or the substitution of human doctrines for the divine reduces religious devotion to hypocrisy, Jesus calls for nothing less than a complete change of heart.

> The things that come out of the mouth come from the heart, and it is these that make a man unclean. For from the heart come evil intentions: murder, adultery, fornication, theft, perjury, slander. These are the things that make a man unclean (Mt 15:18–20).

Thus, Jesus brings to the justice of the Old Testament Law the new dimension of love, requiring not only that the commandments be kept, but that the justice done be leavened with love. In this way, Jesus links acts of justice to growth in holiness. Pope John Paul II clarifies this understanding when he writes:

> A close connection is made between eternal life and obedience to God's commandments: God's commandments show man the path of life and they lead to it. From the very lips of Jesus, the new Moses, man is once again given the commandments of the Decalogue....Jesus brings God's commandments to fulfillment, particularly the commandment of love of neighbor, by interiorizing their demands and by bringing out their fullest meaning. Love of neighbor springs from a loving heart which, precisely because it loves, is ready to live out the loftiest challenges. Jesus shows that the commandments must not be understood as a minimum limit not to be gone beyond, but rather as a path involving a moral and spiritual journey toward perfection, at the heart of which is love.[34]

Legal Justice Determines How We Live as Americans

We live in a nation which closely regulates the behavior of its citizens. While our constitution assures us the freedoms of life, liberty and the pursuit of happiness, we are not wholly free when it comes to the many aspects of everyday living. Our freedom is seriously constrained by our duty to respect the rights of others. Laws and regulations touch every aspect of our daily life.

The United States Code is the official compilation of the federal laws of a general and permanent nature that Americans must obey. The Code is divided into fifty titles; each title is divided into sections, and these are further subdivided.[35] In addition, there are a plethora of federal regulations that must be obeyed like laws, even to no smoking in airplanes and wearing seat belts, as well as state and local laws and ordinances.

The regulations that affect us most intimately are the tax laws; rates vary according to income, so the federal rates can vary between 15% to 39.6% on a person's taxable income. In addition, of course, there are local, state and other federal taxes in accord with tax legislation. Sales taxes also account for a significant portion of income, such taxes garnering from 2% to 8.1% in most jurisdictions.

Every time we drive a vehicle, we are governed by traffic laws. Laws tightly regulate buying and selling, investing, insurance, renting and buying property. All food must be labeled, and alcoholic beverages are strictly controlled. Some medicine can only be purchased with a doctor's prescription, and these medicines have to pass rigid inspection by the Food and Drug Administration. Recent legislation has been passed by Congress which seeks to preserve the environment, and, as a result, strictly limits what both corporations and individuals can do on their property.[36]

Not only are our lives governed by many laws, the laws are constantly being changed; new ones are being added, and old ones are allowed to die. Politics may be defined as the fine art of the possible, but it is actually the fine art of passing as many laws as possible which will be acceptable to the American people. For this purpose, the United States Congress is composed of 435 voting members in the House of Representatives and 100 senators (two from each state). Each session lasts one year during which bills are proposed, debated and passed or not passed.

Some of the laws that are passed are to the advantage of some people and of disadvantage to others. For example, affirmative action was seen as a way of redressing injustices brought about by racial discrimination; subsequently, however, laws requiring quotas were repealed because they were perceived as working against true equality in the job market.[37]

Laws are at the center of the divisions between liberals and conservatives, the religious and non-religious, and sometimes the divisions are very deep and foment great acrimony. The public dialogue over the differences is sometimes marked by name-calling, character assassination, false accusations, mud-slinging and lying. Nevertheless, Catholics are called to witness to justice issues by being reasonably familiar with the issues under discussion and actively engaging in the public dialogues whenever it is appropriate.

While most of the laws of the United States are viewed by the church as just, others are seen as profoundly unjust and deeply disruptive of the common good. Laws permitting abortion are seen as immoral insofar as they permit the killing of innocent babies. Partial-birth abortion which kills the child who has partially emerged from the womb is particularly abhorrent to the Catholic conscience and sensitive humanists.

Catholics clearly have a responsibility to work to change unjust laws, including public protests that can take a variety of forms. Still, doing violence and injuring others and destroying property in the quest for justice is not an acceptable option. So, for example, it is unjust to bomb an abortion clinic, since such extreme violence places even innocent human lives at great risk.

Commutative Justice Directs Human Beings in Their Relations with Others

Commutative justice, like all justice, is also a matter of rights and duties. In this case, it is justice between individuals and is achieved by some form of agreement or contract, explicit or implied, formal or informal, witnessed or not. For example, a wage is just when the payment is commensurate with the amount and quality of the work performed. The "just wage" itself requires a specific determination of the amount that is mutually agreed to by the contracting parties. In the United States, however, we have the minimum wage law to guarantee that the worker gets a fair minimum wage in the light of the economic realities of American society.[38]

The legal standard, which undergoes upgrading from time to time, has been disputed by those saying it is too high as well as by those saying it is too low. In either case, however, both sides are trying to implement in law the principle flowing from the virtue of justice—namely, fairness. And since society has established by law what is just, the employer has the duty to pay the just wage; the determination of the just wage is not left to the individual judgment of either party alone.[39]

Yet, justice may, in fact, require more than meeting the requirements established by legal justice. For example, while a businessman is legally bound to pay the minimum wage to his workers or suffer the legal consequences of non-payment, the virtue of justice which connects him with the glory of God may require him to pay above, even considerably above, the minimum wage in order to be truly fair. Perhaps the employee has a family and the legislated minimum wage is not adequate to provide for the family's needs. The virtue of justice would require the employer to take that economic reality into account in computing a just wage. This would not be an act of charity which an employer would be free to do or not to do; the just wage is a right of the wage-earner. Hence, the virtue of justice may require more than any civil law.[40] At the same time, it can never demand less.

Distributive Justice Regulates the Use of Resources

Scripture tells us that when God created our first parents, he appointed Adam to be the caretaker of all the wonderful things God made on earth.

> Yahweh God took the man and settled him in the garden
> of Eden to cultivate and take care of it (Gen 2:15).

We are increasingly aware that our natural resources are not limitless and that the environment is such a delicately balanced mechanism that even slight disruption of one of its elements can seriously affect the smooth functioning of the whole. Care of the environment raises complex issues which far exceed the competence of the untrained Catholic, no matter how good-willed she or he may be. The just person may actually be found on either side.[41] Because of the complexity of resource issues, justice requires that each side be given a hearing, and if a particular matter is submitted to judicial arbitration, the final decision—when legally upheld—must be respected in justice. One does not have to agree with every decision; indeed, one may work vigorously to have it overturned on appeal. Nevertheless, in the interim, to avoid total anarchy—injustice to the extreme—even unpopular decisions must be honored.

Social Justice and the Popes

Each type of justice—legal, commutative, and distributive—impacts society in varying degrees. Thus, each is, to a certain extent, *social* justice. A great number of social justice cases are concerned with economics and the cultures that result from economic policies. The Catholic Church became a vigorous advocate of social justice as a result of the economic consequences of the industrial revolution. The last decades of the nineteenth century saw the invention and use of more and more powerful machines to accomplish what had been done by hand. From the perspective of social justice, it could be said that the industrial revolution created a vast economic culture that enriched a relative few at the expense of the many locked into poorly paid and stultifying jobs. Arguably, this situation continues today, albeit in a more hi-tech venue, so that economic injustices continue to afflict humankind and enmesh the human spirit in materialistic slavery.

A long succession of popes has addressed the social justice issues created by industrialism; their teachings have developed slowly over the ten decades since Leo XIII's *Rerum Novarum* in 1891. The development has responded to cultural pressures, especially political forces in Europe,[42] yet thanks to outstanding papal leadership the church has made progress in coming to grips with the vastly complicated problems of structures, societies and the rights of the individual and the family. A key evaluation of this progress was expressed in 1987 by Pope John Paul II in his encyclical *Centesimus Annus*, written to commemorate the one hundredth anniversary of *Rerum Novarum* by Leo XIII.

> In Pope Leo XIII's time...the church's right and duty [to preach on social justice] was far from being commonly admitted....The pope's approach in publishing gave the church "citizenship status" as it were amid the changing realities of public life, and this standing would be more fully confirmed later on.[43]

Fundamental Concerns of Social Justice

Three fundamental concerns underlie the social justice teaching of the church: the sanctity of the family, the dignity of human work and the beneficial use of material goods.[44]

> The natural family, stable and monogamous—as fashioned by God and sanctified by Christianity—in which different generations live together, helping each other to acquire greater wisdom and to harmonize personal rights with other social needs, is the basis of society.[45]

The Book of Genesis tells us that God created an abundance of plants, animals, and fish of the sea; and now, thanks to science, we also know that God created a whole complex mineral kingdom. All these things were created good—very good, in fact, and were given to all of us for both our use (to sustain and better human life) and enjoyment (Gen 1:28-29). They were made to be used by every man, woman, and child on the face of the earth—all of Adam's descendants—so that no one would be without. In times of famine food was to be shared generously with those who were starving, and all things necessary were to be given to those who lacked the essentials. The Book of Leviticus (23:22) has special legislation to provide for the poor. When the farmer gathers in his harvest, he is not to strip his field bare. Rather, he is to leave something lying in the field—the imperfectly cut grain, for example, that falls to the ground—in order that poor people or strangers wandering through the field might pick up the stray pieces and use them for food for themselves.[46]

Jesus himself set the example when he fed a hungry crowd of four thousand people:

> And now once again a great crowd had gathered, and they had nothing to eat. So he called his disciples to him and said to them, "I am moved with pity for all these people; they have been with me for three days now and have nothing to eat. If I send them off home hungry they will collapse on the way; some have come a great distance." His disciples replied, "Where could anyone get bread to feed these people in a deserted place like this?" He asked them, "How many loaves do you have?" "Seven," they said. Then he instructed the crowd to sit down on the ground, and he took the seven loaves, and after giving thanks he broke them and handed them to his disciples to distribute; and they distributed them among the crowd. They had a few small fish as well, and over these he said a blessing and ordered them to be distributed also. They ate as much as they wanted, and they

collected seven basketfuls of the scraps left over. Now there had been about four thousand men present, not counting women and children (Mark 8:1-10).[47]

In Matthew (25:31-46) Jesus describes the last judgment where the just are rewarded:

> For I was hungry and you gave me food, I was thirsty and you gave me drink. I was a stranger and you made me welcome, naked and you clothed me, sick and you visited me, in prison and you came to see me.

Need for the very fundamentals of sustaining life is of such great priority that a starving person does no injustice if he is forced to steal from someone who has more food than he needs. (He cannot steal from someone who is starving to the extent that he is, of course.)

This fundamental principle of justice has extensive ramifications even in terms of the relationship of rich nations to the poor nations. No nation has the right to exploit the poverty of the underdeveloped nation for its own economic advancement. On the contrary, it is the duty of the rich and developed nations to help the poor and undeveloped countries to become self-sufficient and able to engage productively in international trade.[48] To this end, it will be necessary for the rich of the world to establish those mechanisms by which such productivity becomes possible and consistent.[49] The Marshall Plan initiated by the United States after the Second World War is an excellent example of a rich nation reestablishing the entire economy of its vanquished foes; it made possible the western world we have today.[50]

An oft-repeated phrase in the church's social justice teaching is the "preferential option for the poor." This is not a call for the redistribution of wealth, as some might have it,[51] nor does its preference for the poor discriminate against the legitimate rights of other groups. Rather, it means that those who have and enjoy the good things of life must be concerned for the less fortunate and see to it that the poor have all they need for a truly human existence.

Pope John Paul II puts it this way:

> This preferential option for the poor [is] never exclusive or discriminatory toward other groups. This option is not limited to material poverty, since it is well known that there are many other forms of poverty, especially in modern society—not only economic, but cultural and spiritual poverty as well. The church's love for the poor, which is essential for her and a part of her constant tradition, impels her to give attention to a world in which poverty is threatening to assume massive proportions in spite of technological and economic progress. In the countries of the west, different forms of poverty are being experienced by groups which live on the margins of society, by the elderly and the sick, by the victims of consumerism, and even more immediately by so many refugees and migrants. In the developing countries, tragic crises loom on the horizon unless internationally coordinated measures are taken before it is too late.[52]

The Right to Private Property Is Another Principle of Social Justice

While all material goods have a communal aspect, at the same time every human being has a right from nature itself (and codified by man-made law) to possess private property.[53] That is, each person has a right to acquire and dispose of material possessions for the individual's exclusive use. Each has a right to own land, houses and furnishings, clothes—all those things which persons can acquire by dint of their own effort, or which they can inherit from their ancestors.[54]

Society has, therefore, a strict duty to ensure that all persons can profit from their personal labor and enjoy its fruits. This means that the state has the duty of respecting this right of personal profit by providing a stable currency, efficient public services and personal safety. These are things we take for granted in the United States, yet there are many nations in the world where political turmoil, outright corruption, or disordered political ideology provides for none of these. Their absence causes immense personal and social hardship and poverty.

At the same time, while society has a responsibility to create a social climate that ensures legitimate economic business development and resultant job opportunities, it must refrain from legislation which would restrict the free initiative of individuals.[55]

For example, it can be argued that communism and socialism seriously restrict the right of an individual to "to be responsible for his own economic well-being and to provide for his family."[56] We see the tragic results of communism and socialism in the former Soviet-dominated societies. These ideologies—seemingly attractive on the surface but fundamentally unjust—have infused in the people a sense of dependency to such an extent that the victims of these forms of government have lost the sense of personal responsibility of providing for themselves and have been left ill-prepared to work for their own economic well-being. The disintegration of communism and other socialist systems has resulted in social, economic and moral destitution.[57]

Similarly, in the United States, we have come to recognize the many evils of what may be called the "welfare state," and both local and federal governments have begun to effect a rebalancing of—that is to say, a redistribution of justice within—the system via a variety of legislative and policy measures. Basically, there is a legislative effort to make people more responsible for their lives and less dependent on the state and federal governments.[58]

The proper place of private property in the life of individuals is put into perspective by the gospel's encouragement of the evangelical counsel of poverty.[59] Since the beginning of the Church, men and women have vowed themselves to apostolic poverty in the imitation of Christ in order to commit themselves more fully to living the Christian life. Nothing is more important in this life or the next than the kingdom of God; the vow of poverty bears witness to this value in a radical way. The Gospel of Luke in particular helps us to understand the value God puts on complete detachment from possessing things when Luke tells the story of a rich young man who came to Jesus and asked him what he had to do to be "perfect." Jesus said to him: "There is still one thing you lack. Sell all that you own and distribute the money to the poor, and you will have treasure in heaven; then come, follow me" (Lk 18:22).

And when the young man refused to follow, Jesus was saddened about the corrupting effect of riches on the human heart. He said: "It is easier for a camel to pass through the eye of a needle than for a rich person to enter the kingdom of God" (Lk 18:25). In fact, Paul attributes the "love of money" as the root of all evil, "and there are some who, pursuing it, have wandered away from the faith, and so given their souls any number of fatal wounds" (1 Tim 6:10).

On the other hand, Jesus commended Peter and the other disciples for giving up everything in this world to follow him. Not only did he commend Peter, he commended everyone throughout future centuries to come who entered what we call "the religious life." He said to them,

> I tell you solemnly, there is no one who has left house, wife, brothers, parents or children for the sake of the kingdom of God who will not be given repayment many times over in this present time and, in the world to come, eternal life (Lk 18:29-30).

Thus, when the Church includes detachment from wealth in its teachings about economic justice, two things become apparent: (1) the transitory character of possessions when compared to the eternal nature of the human person, and (2) the true value of material things that is found only in their relation to promoting human good on earth. If the use of goods impedes justice, then such goods not only have no value, they have a negative value which will have repercussions in this life and the next.

Love Is the Motivation for Social Justice

What distinguishes the church's social gospel from purely secular theory is the central place love has in the execution of just policies, not only in the economic arena, but in all human relations. The reason for this centrality of love is the death of Jesus Christ.

> He was bearing our faults in his own body on the cross,
> so that we might die to our faults and live for holiness;
> through his wounds you have been healed (1 Pet 2:24).

This great love of Jesus which caused him to die for us is the model of our own love for one another. As Jesus said, "This is my commandment: love one another as I have loved you" (Jn 15:12).

A marvelous passage from the Gospel of Luke most succinctly and forcefully reveals both the centrality and the extent of love in Catholic life. We are to love our enemies, do good to those who hate us and bless them. At the very least, we are to pray for them. In fact, we are to help them when they abuse us or rob us. We are to give freely. In short, we are to treat others as we would like to have them treat us. Our reward will come if we are compassionate, and kind, even to the ungrateful. In short, "the amount you measure out is the amount you will be given back" (Lk 6:27–38).

Christ-like love can never take the place of justice; it builds on justice, and without justice there can be no love. With this understanding of love, Pope John Paul II explains how this is lived out in the life of the church today:

> As far as the church is concerned, the social message of the gospel must not be considered a theory, but above all else a basis and a motivation for action. Inspired by this message, some of the first Christians distributed their goods to the poor, bearing witness to the fact that despite different social origins it was possible for people to live together in peace and harmony. Through the power of the gospel, down through the centuries monks tilled the land, men and women religious founded hospitals and shelters for the poor, and confraternities as well as individual men and women of all states of life devoted themselves to the needy and to those on the margins of society, convinced as they were that Christ's words "As you did it to one of the least of these my brethren, you did it to me" (Mt 25:40) were not intended to remain a pious wish, but were meant to become a concrete life commitment.[60]

In the Metro stations in Washington there was a stark, black and white photograph of a homeless woman staring out to the camera. Underneath, there was a bold message: "The homeless have a face." Perhaps this better than anything else reflects the teaching of John Paul II when he writes:

> Love for others, and in the first place love for the poor, in whom the church sees Christ himself, is made concrete in the promotion of justice. Justice will never be fully attained unless people see in the poor person, who is asking for help in order to survive, not an annoyance or a burden, but an opportunity for showing kindness and a chance for greater enrichment.[61]

The Heart of Social Justice for Catholics Is the Vote

A virtue so closely connected to justice that it is called by St. Thomas a potential part of justice, or, better, an adjunct virtue to justice, is liberality[62]. The proper act of liberality is the generous use of money, the unselfish giving up of one's time and the using of one's talents creatively for the benefit of others. This virtue is a great source of strength for the Catholic parish when it comes to working for social justice on all levels.

To work for social justice, particularly when one runs into opposition, requires a disposition of mind to expend oneself for others, and that without hope of reward. In a particular way, then, liberality is the virtue by which one vigorously exerts oneself in political action to achieve the end of justice. To turn out the vote on justice issues requires a great expenditure of time, creative energy and money. Yet such hard and demanding work is necessary in order to win individual voters to the side of justice in local, state and federal elections.[63]

The parish formation team, therefore, enjoys great influence in bringing about social justice because of the power of the single vote. This single vote is more influenced by one's immediate family, friends and local church than by politicians' speeches, campaigns and newspaper and television editorials. The "grass roots" is a political and social reality that has great power when it is properly channeled. Here the individual's holiness makes the difference in the way the United States is run and the values which it encapsulates in law. No matter where else the parish has influence, it certainly has great influence at the "grass roots."

The United States government—a democracy based (broadly) on the concept of "one man–one vote"—is the forum where the broadest aspects of social justice are legislated. Catholics therefore have both a unique opportunity and a special obligation to express their conscience, through the exercise of their right to vote, regarding the justice issues in all levels of society (e.g., immigration, race, gender, economic and political policies, life and medical ethics, the environment, etc.). Because of the complexity of these issues as well as the division of opinion concerning how these issues are to be treated, observing the principle of subsidiarity[64], the appropriate level of society — federal, state or local government, the parish, etc.—needs to identify the problems and provide just answers for the questions they raise.

The power of one vote is particularly evident on the local level. This same local level most intimately touches the lives of the inhabitants. Witness, for example, how the policies of a school board impact so forcefully on the education of children in a particular school district. Membership in a parent-teacher organization is another effective way of influencing local policies, as is membership on local hospital boards. Judges are often, if not usually, elected and wield great power during their term of office.

While all the levels of government of the United States depend for day-to-day operations on dedicated career public servants who constitute a vast bureaucracy, the principal agents in government at the diverse levels are appointed by elected officials. Even judges are appointed to the Supreme Court by the President and Congress, and the ones in office, as a result of their election by the voters, strive to appoint those persons sympathetic to the political point of view that got them elected. Furthermore, the laws that govern the activities of the various governmental agencies are conceived by elected representatives. Thus, in a very true sense, the American electorate has the ultimate responsibility for the laws and regulations under which we live. The decision about who should be elected is crucial, and thus the casting of each individual vote is a grave duty in justice.

The Specific Ministry of the Parish Formation Team Is To Lead Individual Persons to Holiness

Pope John Paul II saw that the individual person is enmeshed in complicated interrelationships with other individuals and indeed with the whole of society, yet, at the same time, the person remains a single individual, infinitely precious in the sight of God.[65] Consequently, although the church's social teaching draws on the insights of the secular sciences to help individuals, families and even nations achieve their rights, ultimately the church aims at bringing to each person the salvation offered by Jesus Christ through the proclamation of the gospel. Everything that the Church does in the area of social justice, it does as part of this proclamation, thereby avoiding the trap of social and moral relativism.[66]

Life in society has neither the market economy nor the state as its final purpose, since life itself has a unique value which the state and the market must serve. The human person remains above all a being who seeks the truth and strives to live in that truth, deepening his or her understanding of it through a dialogue which involves past and future.[67]

Catholic social teaching is solidly founded on the premise that, no matter how powerful they may be, human beings are never fully controlled by the diverse forces in society. Without a doubt these forces have great influence, but the human person—who has been created in the image of God—is free and has the responsibility of contributing to society's moral development in the same measure that he has been given the gift of participation in the revelation of Christ. The martyrs are the greatest witnesses to this counter-cultural freedom.[68]

In fact, the person of faith is the primary vehicle through which the church transforms society and brings forth Christian justice to all—believers or not. The individual Christian is a minister of evangelization. Paul VI wrote one of the most important documents of the contemporary church with his *Apostolic Exhortation on Evangelization (Evangelii Nuntiandi)*. In that document he speaks movingly about how renewal in society can be effected only by persons who are themselves renewed with gospel power.

> There is no new humanity if there are not first of all new persons renewed by baptism and by lives according to the gospel. The purpose of evangelization is therefore precisely this interior change, and if it had to be expressed in one sentence, the best way of stating it would be to say that the church evangelizes when she seeks to convert, solely through the divine power of the message she proclaims, both the personal and collective consciences of people, the activities in which they engage, and the lives and concrete milieux which are theirs.[69]

Subsidiarity Preserves Individual and Local Community Freedom

Pope John XXIII forcefully taught that although society has an essential role in the ordering of events to assure or bring about social justice, at the same time, within society's activities, a certain order is to prevail which observes the principle of *subsidiarity*.[70]

> Just as it is wrong to withdraw from the individual and commit to a community what private enterprise and industry can accomplish, so too it is an injustice, a grave evil and a disturbance of right order for a larger and higher association to arrogate to itself functions which can be performed efficiently by smaller and lower societies. Of its very nature the true aim of all social activity should be to help members of the social body, but never to destroy or absorb them.[71]

So, for example, the individual workers are the first to regulate their mutual relations where their work is concerned.

> If they cannot do so, or will not do so, then, and only then, does it fall back on the state to intervene in the division and distribution of work, and this must be according to the form and measure that the common good properly understood, demands.[72]

While Pope John XXIII raised the issue of subsidiarity in 1961, Pope John Paul II refined this notion and applied it specifically to the rise of the welfare state. He acknowledges that in some countries greater intervention by the state has been required to assure the well-being of the populace, at the same time also emphasizing that such intervention has also given rise to grave abuse.[73]

Needs are best understood and satisfied by people who are closest to them and who act as neighbors to those in need. It should be added that certain kinds of demands often call for a response which is not simply material, but which is capable of perceiving the deeper human need. One thinks of the condition of refugees, immigrants, the elderly, the sick, and all those in circumstances which call for assistance, such as drug abusers. All these people can be helped effectively only by those who offer them genuine fraternal support, in addition to the necessary care.

An example of this are hospices run by private charitable organizations or churches which stress the interpersonal aspects of care and dying. Local parishes and communities are best able to supply the kind of fraternal and familial support that gives the personal touch to all treatment and care.

The Parish Forms Christ's Disciples for Justice

The perspectives that govern a nation in its efforts to promote justice, especially in a democracy such as the United

States, come primarily from the individuals who constitute the citizenry of the country. Pope Paul VI calls the individual believers who affect the justice issues "leaven." They are the leaven of the gospel[74] because it is in the home and family that individuals first enter into relationships with others and learn how to be just and to respect the rights and dignity of others. When these lessons are taught well, and well learned, they set the course for the entire society.[75] Christians' specific contribution to justice is the day-to-day life of the individual believer acting like the leaven of the gospel in his family, his school, his work and his social and civic life. Included with this are the perspectives and meaning which the faithful can give to human effort. As stated by the Roman Synod in *Justice in the World* (1971):

> [E]ducation demands a renewal of heart, a renewal based on the recognition of sin in its individual and social manifestations....Since this education makes men decidedly more human, it will help them to be no longer the object of manipulation by communications media or political forces....Education for justice is imparted first in the family. We are well aware that not only church institutions but also other schools, trade unions and political parties are collaborating in this....The content of this education necessarily involves respect for the person and for his dignity. Since it is world justice which is in question here, the unity of the human family within which, according to God's plan, a human being is born must first of all be seriously affirmed. Christians find a sign of this solidarity in the fact that all human beings are destined to become in Christ sharers in the divine nature.[76]

Education for justice does not end in the home. The church, unions, civic organizations, and schools all have a role in forming the citizenry of a country for justice. Since justice is a very personal virtue, it is most appropriate that it be fostered in human persons by other human persons working together. The gospel, moreover, gives a powerful perspective for examining the issues of human justice and injustice in the world today.[77]

Justice: The Bedrock for Holiness

Unless Catholics are fundamentally just in all their dealings with government, organizations and other human beings, they cannot make progress in growing in holiness. There is no real love without justice, and no holiness without love. To grow in holiness requires not that we as individuals meet a specific set of external criteria, but that we possess—strive to possess—the internal faith connection that binds us to Christ and opens our hearts to his good news. Then, and only then, can we go forth to join hands with our fellow men and women to build a just society.

Epilogue

*J*ust before he ascended into heaven, Jesus appeared one last time to his disciples. He left them with a final command that has transformed the world, saying:

> All power in heaven and on earth has been given to me. Go, therefore, and make disciples of all nations, baptizing them in the name of the Father, and of the Son, and of the Holy Spirit, teaching them to observe all that I have commanded you. And behold, I am with you always, until the end of time (Mt 28:18-20).

This is the great commission Jesus gave to his church, a commission the church has faithfully carried out for some two thousand years among all the peoples and cultures of the world. Carrying out this great commission is the "essential mission of the church." Furthermore, "it is a task and mission which the vast and profound changes of present-day society make all the more urgent."[1]

The Parish Team Is Central to Renewal

While all Christians are called to witness, Jesus' commission falls in a special way and with a special urgency on those who have been called by God to form others in the faith. The task is most clear in parents, the first preachers of the faith, and their families, a task that "precedes, accompanies and enriches all other forms of catechesis."[2] It is equally clear that this is the task of the ordained: bishops, priests and deacons. Finally it is the clear task of those who have willingly answered the call of God to become part of the parish formation team—those men and women who, under the leadership of their bishop and pastor, serve as evangelists, catechists and administrators. Since the Council of Trent, the territorial parish has been and remains the center of all Catholic life. After the Second Vatican Council, many "experimental parishes" were established to provide new and innovative approaches to both liturgy and catechesis. Usually they had broken off in whole or part from a territorial parish, seemingly to answer better the needs of the people who formed them. The movement, however, did not have a long life. The new gatherings of people lacked the necessary stability for the long haul, and, probably more importantly, they lacked the diversity of personalities and gifts that mark the traditional parish. Today the parish has returned to its rightful place at the center of Catholic life.

Pope John Paul II says that in the light of its centrality, the parish

> must rediscover its vocation, which is to be a fraternal and welcoming family home, where those who have been baptized and confirmed become aware of forming the people of God. In that home, the bread of good doctrine and the eucharistic bread are broken for them in abundance, in the setting of the one act of worship; from that home they are sent out day by day to their apostolic mission in all the centers of activity of the life of the world.[3]

At the very heart of the vocation of the parish is the experience of the good news as a liberating power which gives both joy and peace to all those who believe. Since this is so, good news spirituality is also the heart of the ministries of the parish team, whatever forms they take. Parish ministries, paid or volunteer, are not jobs; they are answers to the call of God to serve his people. Since it is a call of God, the team can be sure that God gives each member the grace for the diverse ministries to build up the body of Christ. There are graces for evangelists, others for pastors and teachers, certainly for parents, and, yes, for children and the whole family as well. All these special graces from the Holy Spirit equip the holy ones for the work of ministry, for building up the body of Christ. Each part of the body, working in graceful harmony with all the other parts, brings about the body's growth as it builds itself up in love (cf. Eph 4:1-14).

If the whole Bible cannot encompass totally the mystery of salvation, certainly no single book about the spirituality of the good news can do it. Nevertheless, I have attempted, with the help of so many men and women of faith to whom I am deeply grateful, to provide a basic reference point, "an attainable vision of holiness in such a way that each will hunger to be holy."[4] Because we are made in the image of God, and God is holy, a vision of holiness allows men and women of good will to see the teachings of Christ as the good news of freedom, joy and peace. This vision of holiness needs to be revitalized in our Catholic parishes because we live in a world and an age that has lost its Judeo-Christian heritage of the revealed truth of God and instead has been lured into putting faith into a variety of human myths that are passed off as truth.[5]

There is so much evidence, as I have pointed out, that these other ways are not bringing the joy, peace and the sure self-identity they promise, but rather have plunged men and women into personal and social chaos. Hence, the importance of the team's ministry to proclaim God's own truth as revealed in the scriptures and tradition and passed on in the church.

As we come to the end of this series of reflections on holiness and its consequences, aside from an underlying attitude or mind-set, the question remains: Are there specific ways to incarnate this basic vision in the parish? As very practical people, we like to figure out what specifically is to be done. Are there programs or approaches that should be added to the already many and diverse ministries in a parish? Maybe nothing needs to be added, but perhaps a reexamination of existing ministries in the light of what I have been suggesting in this book might be helpful.

The Sunday Eucharist Reflects the Faith of the Parish

Since Sunday Mass is for most practicing Catholics their principal, if not only, contact with the community life of the parish, the team might find it valuable to review the eucharistic celebrations to see if they really are celebrations. That is, is the manner of celebration one which reflects communal joy in the Lord? The *Constitution on the Sacred Liturgy* addresses pastors:

> When the liturgy is celebrated, more is required than the mere observance of the laws governing valid and licit celebration. It is [the pastors'] duty to ensure that the faithful take part knowingly, actively, and fruitfully.[6]

Throughout this book we have been proposing certain basic attitudes—such as gratitude for gifts received—that enable the people of God to truly give thanks and celebrate. In addition, the team should ascertain if all the elements in the liturgy accurately symbolize the interior dispositions of the worshipers to praise God.

Parish Devotions Contribute to a Sense of the Holy

When the Second Vatican Council renewed the liturgy of the church, it focused on the sacraments, and especially on the eucharistic liturgy. But it did not intend, as some have suggested, that popular devotions and sacramentals should be discouraged or abolished. In the *Constitution on the Sacred Liturgy* the Council specifically encouraged popular devotions as a way of strengthening participation in the public liturgy of the church.

> Popular devotions of the Christian people, provided they conform to the laws and norms of the church, are to be highly recommended....Such devotions should be so drawn up that they harmonize with the liturgical seasons, accord with the sacred liturgy, are in some way derived from it, and lead the people to it, since in fact the liturgy by its very nature is far superior to any of them.[7]

The council goes on to give the reason for recommending such devotions in n. 60 of the same Constitution, asserting that sacramentals dispose people of faith to receive the chief effects of the sacraments, and various occasions in life are thereby rendered holy. That Constitution deepens our appreciation of the power of sacramentals when it states:

> The divine grace of the sacraments and sacramentals flows from the paschal mystery of the passion, death and resurrection of Christ....There is scarcely any proper use of material things which cannot thus be directed toward the sanctification of men and the praise of God.[8]

The church has fostered many beautiful devotions throughout its long history, and these devotions have brought great comfort and strength to those who use them. In particular, the parish team should actively promote devotion to Mary, especially by the recitation of the rosary, if not in public, at least in private when it is difficult to offer other forms of prayer.

Parish-sponsored pilgrimages, too, can bring great graces to the parish community. One has only to see the outpouring of fervor in places like Lourdes or St. Anne de Beaupré to recognize the power of prayer in the lives of the suffering.

Recently I preached a novena to St. Jude. Each night the church was filled with six to eight hundred people calling on St. Jude for help in their desperate cases. During the novena, in addition to a substantial homily and appropriate prayers, we had benediction of the Most Blessed Sacrament and venerated a relic of St. Jude. Afterward, a number of people came up to me to tell me of the special favors they had received through the intercession of St. Jude. The same church was bright with vigil candles burning before statues of Mary and St. Joseph as well as before the special shrine of St. Jude. At each sacred image, the faithful were rapt in prayer.

Who has not been impressed by the crowds turning out to receive ashes on Ash Wednesday, or to make the Stations of the Cross, especially during Lent? From time to time parishes will celebrate the venerable "Forty Hours," replete with preaching, processions and adoration of the Blessed Eucharist. It is a time of great joy as the parish finds a renewed identity around the living body and blood of Christ.

Not every devotion appeals to everyone, which is precisely why the church provides such a variety of options. The fact, however, that non-liturgical services attract so many pious men and women from all walks of life and with varying degrees of faith is a powerful witness to Catholics' comfort with their saints in the great communion of saints. Fostering such devotions, therefore, becomes a real service the parish team can render to the faithful as it helps individuals grow in holiness even as the team builds up the body of Christ.

Hospitality Is the Witness of the Parish Community

Connected closely with eucharistic celebration and the devotional life is a spirit of hospitality which should so permeate the parish in all its activities that both Catholics and others outside the church can recognize the loving presence of Christ in the midst of the church. Hospitality would include social activities as well as educational and spiritual gatherings. Hospitality would also include the ease with which parochial services are available, even in such simple things as the answering and returning of telephone calls. Hospitality includes giving inquirers information about the different ministries and helping them to make contact with the persons in charge.

Perhaps specially prepared teams of evangelists in addition to the usual catechetical team could be added if they are not already present. From the chapter on social justice, it is clear that the parish should have definite programs to promote social justice on the local, state and even national level. And, of course, the parish itself should be sensitive to social justice in its own policies regarding wages, salaries and benefits.

The Bible Is a Rich Source of Parish Renewal

There are two final reflections I offer to be considered in the reexamination. First, in the light of my own pastoral experience of preaching Bible missions in hundreds of parishes throughout the United States and Canada for over twenty years, I suggest that parishes, schools, families and individuals give greater emphasis to the Bible. Pope Paul VI expressed the reason for a renewed emphasis on the Bible when he wrote:

> The holy task of spreading God's word to the widest possible readership has a special urgency today. Despite all his material achievements, man still struggles with the age-old problems of how to order his life for the glory of God, for the welfare of his fellows and for the salvation of his soul. Therefore, we are gratified to find in this new translation of the scriptures a new opportunity for men to give themselves to frequent reading of, and meditation on, the living word of God. In its pages we recognize his voice, and we hear a message of deep significance for

every one of us. Through the spiritual dynamism and prophetic force of the Bible, the Holy Spirit spreads his light and his warmth over all men, in whatever historical or sociological situation they find themselves.[9]

In this the pope is only restating in contemporary terms what the apostle Paul wrote to his beloved Timothy. In his second letter, after describing the evils of the "present age" that is our age, he urged Timothy to read and study the sacred scriptures which he had read even as a child, learning the faith from his mother and grandmother. Then Paul goes on to give the reason for the importance of knowing the sacred writings, which has immediate application for anyone who seeks to work on behalf of the church:

> All scripture is inspired by God and is useful for teaching, for correcting error and for guiding people's lives to bring them to holiness. This is how the person dedicated to God becomes fully prepared and ready for any good work (2 Tim 3:16-17).

Personal Witness Is Essential in Ministry

The second final reflection I would offer is the crucial importance of personal witness in everything the team does. Pope Paul VI asks: "In the long run, is there any other way of handing on the gospel than by transmitting to another person one's personal experience of faith?"[10] The reason the pope gives for such an assertion is: "Modern man listens more willingly to witnesses than to teachers, and if he does listen to teachers, it is because they are witnesses."[11]

For the apostle Paul, the witness of his life was a major source of authority for his preaching to the Corinthians. The little church there was wracked by division and discord, and Paul himself was attacked by some of the church members. The great argument he used against his opponents was the fact that he had suffered more on behalf of the gospel than any of his detractors. He cited his numerous imprisonments, beatings, and brushes with death. He was whipped and beaten and even suffered being stoned, like Stephen. As if that were not enough, Paul was shipwrecked on his sea travels, not once, but three times, and when he was on land he was in constant danger from the travel itself, robbers, and the constant threat of attack by "false brethren." Yet through all this he continued to work on behalf of the gospel; his only real anxiety was for the welfare of his churches, for which he constantly prayed. So powerful was this witness that it is recorded for our sakes in Paul's Second Letter to the Corinthians (11:23-28).

Therefore, in the light of his personal experience, Paul has another message for us of particular value today as we seek to help people grow in the holiness, joy and peace of the Catholic faith. He says:

> Do not be ashamed of your testimony to our Lord, but join with me in suffering for the gospel according to the power of God. He saved us and called us to a holy life, not according to our works but according to his own plan and the grace bestowed on us in Christ Jesus from all eternity (2 Tim 1:8-9).

I Pray for My New Friends

Whenever a reader picks up a book, he or she honors the author by being willing to enter into dialogue with that author: to read his words and to consider them in the light of his or her own life. Finally, the reader may even stick with the author until the bitter end. If you have stayed with me, you honor me. Although I do not know you personally, you have come to know me, and I hope that I have become in some way your friend in Christ Jesus.

So, even if I don't know you, I, as your friend, pray for you the prayer Paul offered for his beloved Ephesians:

> May Christ live in your hearts through faith, and may you be planted in love and built on love. With all God's holy people may you have the strength to grasp the breadth and the length, the height and the depth of the mystery of God's revelation. May you know the love of Christ, which is beyond knowledge. May you be filled with the utter fullness of God. Glory be to God whose power, working in us, can do infinitely more than we can ask or imagine; glory be to him from generation to generation in the church and in Christ Jesus for ever and ever. Amen (Eph 3:14-20).

Notes

INTRODUCTION

1. Cf. John Burke, O.P., and Thomas P. Doyle, O.P., *The Homilist's Guide to Scripture, Theology and Canon Law* (New York: Pueblo Press, 1987). This is a comprehensive treatment of the theology of preaching that underlies this present work.

2. *Code of Canon Law* (1983), Can. 766.

3. Cans. 759, 761.

4. John Paul II, "On Catechesis in Our Time *(Catechesi tradendi)*" *(Origins,* Vol. 9, n. 21, Nov. 8, 1979). "The Task Concerns Us All," nn. 62–68.

5. Vatican Council II, *Declaration on Christian Education,* n. 3 (October 28, 1965).

6. Pope John Paul II, *Veritatis Splendor* (Vatican City: Libreria Editrice Vaticana, 1993).

7. While holiness is always dependent upon human effort, it is also always a gift that is conferred by God ordinarily through the ministry of Christ's church. The gift of grace moves the believer to those decisions and acts which make him or her holy. The role of grace in this is explained more fully in a subsequent chapter. See also *Catechism of the Catholic Church,* 2013.

8. Obviously this is a very brief treatment of a topic that deserves greater consideration. Three books in particular can be of help in understanding both the influence and the pervasiveness of these principles as they affect the preaching of the gospel of Jesus

Christ and the establishment of Christian moral principles. Reference will be made to them in later chapters.

(a) Robert N. Bellah, et al., *Habits of the Heart: Individualism and Commitment in American Life* (Berkeley: University of California Press, 1985). A well-researched and perceptively written sociological study of the contemporary American character. Especially helpful when read in conjunction with Vitz (below).

(b) Allan Bloom, *The Closing of the American Mind: How Higher Education Has Failed Democracy and Impoverished the Souls of Today's Education* (New York: Simon and Schuster, 1987). A brilliant analysis of why young Americans think the way they do; it contains obvious implications for preaching in today's society.

(c) Paul C. Vitz, *Psychology as Religion: The Cult of Self-Worship* (Grand Rapids: Wm. B. Erdmans, 1977). A most helpful book for coming to understand the psychological milieux of contemporary America.

9. This is developed by the noted psychiatrist, Karl Menninger, M.D., in his informative book, *Whatever Became of Sin?* (New York: Hawthorn Books, Inc., 1973).

10. Some moralists today propose "love" as the sole norm for morality that always obliges. But this leaves "love" undefined. Jesus does indeed say that love of God and neighbor is the greatest commandment (Mk 12:31), but he also insists on the other commandments as well. These other commandments define what *true* love is (Mt 5:17).

Actually, throughout the whole Bible the norm of morality is more often named "holiness" than love, although true holiness and true love are identical, since God is both holiness and love. To avoid the ambiguity of "love" in today's language, in this book I have preferred to base all Christian morality on imaging the holiness of God.

For an excellent treatment of some contemporary theories see *Moral Theology Today: Certitudes and Doubts* (St. Louis: The Pope John XXIII Medical-Moral Research and Education Center, 1984). Chapter 8 is particularly germane to contemporary understandings of love.

11. Pope John Paul II in his encyclical *Veritatis Splendor* has forcefully reaffirmed the validity of the Church's traditional doctrine regarding mortal sin: "With every freely committed mortal sin, he

offends God as the giver of the Law and as a result becomes guilty with regard to the entire Law (cf. Jas 2:8-11); even if he perseveres in faith, he loses 'sanctifying grace,' 'charity' and 'eternal happiness.' As the Council of Trent teaches, 'the grace of justification once received is lost not only by apostasy, by which faith itself is lost, but also by any other mortal sin.'" John Paul II, *Veritatis Splendor* (Vatican City: Libreria Editrice Vaticana, 1993), n. 68. See especially nn. 68-70.

12. This is why every Mass we celebrate begins with a confession of sin.

1. THE PERSPECTIVE OF THE
AMERICAN CATHOLIC LISTENER

1. Robert N. Bellah, *et al.*, *Habits of the Heart: Individualism and Commitment in American Life* (Berkeley: University of California Press, 1985), 228.

2. *Ibid.*, 229.

3. *Ibid.*, 226.

4. *Ibid.*, 221.

5. George Gallup, Jr. and Jim Castelli, *The American Catholic People: Their Beliefs, Practices and Values* (New York: Doubleday & Company, Inc., 1987), 65.

6. *Ibid.*, 48.

7. *Ibid.*, 77.

8. *Ibid.*, 67.

9. What is perhaps of most interest in 1993 is that neither the bishops' peace pastoral nor their economic pastoral is familiar to the vast majority of Catholics: 18% are familiar with the former, 19% with the latter. Only the pastoral on women, which was never issued, is in the Catholic consciousness, with 44% of Catholics knowing about that. *U.S. Catholicism: Trends in the '90's* (National Catholic Reporter/Gallup Poll Supplement, October 8, 1993), 30.

10. Gallup, *op. cit.*, 104.

11. David C. Leege, *Catholics and the Civic Order: Parish Participation, Politics, and Civic Participation,* Research Report, No. 11 (Notre Dame: Notre Dame Study of Catholic Life, October, 1987), 11.

12. *Ibid.*, 12.

13. Unpublished lecture in a workshop, Dominican Preaching Today (June 4, 1987).

14. *Origins* (Washington, DC: NC Documentary News Service, October 1, 1987; Vol. 17, No. 16), 259.

15. Gallup, *op. cit.*, 43.

16. "Why Catholics Stay in the Church," in *America* (August 1-8, 1987; Vol. 157, No. 3), 54.

17. *Ibid.*, 55.

18. *Ibid.*, 42.

19. The observations recorded in this section are taken from *U.S. Catholicism: Trends in the '90's,* National Catholic Reporter/Gallup Poll NCR/Gallup Poll Supplement (October 8, 1993), 21-31. It is a follow up to the NCR/Gallup Poll taken in May 1987.

20. *Ibid.*, 26.

21. *Ibid.*, 29.

22. *Ibid.*, 30.

23. Edward Schillebeeckx, *Church: The Human Story of God* (New York: Crossroad, 1990), 50.

24. *Origins, op. cit.*, 261.

25. *Ibid.*, 260.

26. *Op. cit.*, 261.

27. "The program of our collegial ministry cannot be other than to release into the life stream of ecclesial life all the richness of the church's self-understanding, which was given by the Holy Spirit to the community of faith in the celebration of the Second Vatican Council....At the heart of the church's self-understanding is the notion of *communion:* primarily a sharing through grace in the life of the Father given us through Christ and in the Holy Spirit." Pope John Paul II to the Bishops of the United States, September 16, 1987 in *Origins, op. cit.*, 257.

28. *Catechism of the Catholic Church.* Vatican City: Libreria Editrice Vaticana, 1994. This abbreviation is used for the document throughout this book; the numbers refer to the paragraphs as enumerated in the *Catechism.*

29. Although the story of the fall is narrated only once in the scriptures, the universal sinfulness of humanity antecedent to personal sin which it initiated is asserted or assumed throughout the

Bible. When St. Augustine was battling against the Pelagians, who denied the reality of original sin, he developed this doctrine by appealing to both scripture and the church's practice of baptizing infants. See Karl Rahner, ed., "Original Sin," in *Encyclopedia of Theology* (New York: Seabury Press, 1975), 1148–1155.

30. Pope John Paul II specifies this original sin in *Veritatis Splendor:* "With this imagery, revelation teaches that *the power to decide what is good and what is evil does not belong to man, but to God alone*" (n. 35). Emphasis in the original.

2. THE HOLINESS OF GOD

1. "Abram" was the one called by God. It was not until later, when the Lord made the covenant with him, that "Abram" received the name "Abraham" (Gen 17:5). I have used the name that matches the scriptural text.

2. According to Genesis 4:26, in primitive times the divine name "Yahweh" had been known to Enoch and others.

3. This theme of the infallible efficacy of the divine will permeates all of scripture. It is the basis of God's faithfulness to those with whom he shares his glory. This revelation is particularly apparent in the prophets Amos and Ezekiel. Romans 8:28–30 is especially moving. Hebrews and Ephesians are additional important sources for this teaching. See also Philippians 2:12,13.

4. A reluctance to follow the call of God is clearly not a modern phenomenon, and God continues to be as patient today as he was with Moses. Cf. 2 Peter 3:9: "[The Lord] is patient with you all, wanting nobody to be lost and everybody to be brought to change his ways."

5. John E. Huesdman, S.J., writing on the Book of Exodus in *The Jerome Biblical Commentary,* 3:36.

6. In Deuteronomy, the Sabbath legislation receives a different emphasis which is less immediately related to the holiness of God and, therefore, the holiness of this day. Deuteronomy insists that no work may be done on the Sabbath by anyone, including slaves, animals and aliens, so that everyone can "rest as you do." "For remember that you too were once slaves in Egypt, and the Lord, your God, brought you from there with his strong hand and outstretched

arm. That is why the Lord, your God, has commanded you to observe the Sabbath Day" (Dt 15:1. 15).

7. For example, in regard to food, Leviticus 11:44-45 says they are to avoid eating "swarming creatures that crawl on the ground."

8. Frederick L. Moriarity, S.J., writing on the Book of Numbers in *The Jerome Biblical Commentary* (Englewood Cliffs: Prentice-Hall, Inc., 1968), 5:36. The whole explanation is worth reading.

9. Not all scholars agree on this. John W. Miller, for example, sees it as a characterization by Deutero-Isaiah of his own life as a prophet. Cf. John W. Miller, *Meet the Prophets* (New York: Paulist Press, 1987), 224.

10. John Paul II, *Fides et Ratio*, n. 18. This is one of three rules he gives to the philosopher if "reason were to be fully true to itself" (*Origins*, October 22, 1998: Vol. 28, n. 19, p. 324)

11. See especially Wis 1:3-5; 3:1-12; 7:7-14; 9:1-18.

12. "To all who did accept him, he gave power to become children of God, to all who believe in [his] name" (Jn 1:12).

13. Cf. Jn 6:44.

14. Faith, according to St. Thomas Aquinas, is an assent to something that is not evident in itself because the will wishes to assent. This movement is either because the will orders the assent on account of a good, or because the intellect is convinced by evidence other than the thing itself. Applying that to the devils, it is not because they wanted to believe (which would be an act of meritorious faith), but because they were compelled by the evidence surrounding Jesus. Cf. *ST* II-II, q. 5, a. 2.

15. See also Mark 1:34 where Jesus does not allow the "many devils" to speak "because they knew who he was."

16. By the use of this expression, the writer of the Gospel of John is calling attention to the intimate relation of Jesus to the Father. In the Old Testament, God revealed himself to his people through his prophets as the utterly unique eternal Being. See, for example, Is 41:4: I, Yahweh, who am the first and shall be with the last." See also Dt 32:39; Is 43:13; 46:4; 48:12.

17. *The New Jerusalem Bible* and *The New American Bible, Revised* both translate "the Son of God." *The New American Bible*

considers the statement an affirmation of Christ's divinity, *The New Jerusalem Bible* an affirmation of Christ being more than human. In either case, however, Jesus' holiness in meeting death is clearly declared.

18. To appreciate the impact of this, John 15:8-15 should be read in its entirety.

3. GRACE IS HOLINESS SHARED

1. *CCC* 1996, 2001, 2003, 2021.
2. *CCC* 268-274, 275-78.
3. Cf. Gen 1:31.
4. "I am God unrivaled, God who has no like. From the beginning I foretold the future, and predicted beforehand what is to be. I say: My purpose shall last; I will do whatever I choose. I call a bird of prey from the east, my man of destiny from a far country. No sooner is it said than done, no sooner planned than performed" (Is 46:10-11).
5. God made human beings in the beginning, and then left them free to make their own decisions. If you wish, you can keep the commandments; to be obedient is within your power. He has set fire and water before you; put out your hand to whichever you prefer. You have life and death before you; whichever you like better will be given you. For vast is the wisdom of the Lord; he is almighty and all-seeing. His eyes are on those who fear him; he is aware of every human action. He never commanded anyone to be a sinner; he has given no permission to sin (Sir 15:14-21).
6. *CCC* 600, 2002, 2062.
7. All our good actions are ordered to God; this requires God's grace. On the other hand, not to order actions to God is not a positive motion of being; it is a lack that is not a created reality. Now God provides the physical movement that makes the act possible, but he is not responsible for the twist it takes toward evil which is a privation of order to the proper end. Cf. *ST* I, q. 19, a. 9; I, q. 49, a. 1 and 2.
8. Cf. Eph 1:3-14.
9. "He is the image of the unseen God and the first-born of all creation, for in him were created all things in heaven and on earth: everything visible and everything invisible, thrones, dominations,

sovereignties, powers—all things were created through him and for him. Before anything was created, he existed, and he holds all things in unity. Now the church is his body, he is the head. As he is the beginning, he was the first-born from the dead, so that he should be first in every way, because God wanted all perfection to be found in him and all things to be reconciled through him and for him, everything in heaven and everything on earth, when he made peace by his death on the cross" (Col 1:15-20).

10. Saint Thomas explains that God, being pure act, is incapable of change or increment; he is eternal. As eternal, he sees all things as always present to him ("Aeternitas est tota simul") (*ST* I, q. 10, a. 4). Furthermore, God knows the things he has created not only insofar as they have existence, but also insofar as they have their own determined natures (*ST* I, q. 14, a. 5 & 6). Furthermore, God knows them in himself since his own essence contains all other essences as their cause. Thus, he knows future contingents, or the future (*ST* I, q. 14, a. 13). On the other hand, we can know things only insofar as we perceive them through our senses or arrive at truth through discursive reasoning. Cf. *ST* I, 14, a. 5 and 6. See also Heb 4:12-13; *CCC* 733.

11. *CCC* 221.

12. Cf. Col 1:25-28.

13. *CCC* 1821, 2008-09.

14. *CCC* 688, 2690.

15. Cf. Gal 5:13-26.

16. St. John writes of Jesus: "To all who accept him, he gave power to become children of God, to all who believe in the name of him, who was born not out of human stock, or urge of the flesh, or will of man, but of God himself. The Word was made flesh. He lived among us, and we saw his glory, the glory that is his as the only Son of the Father, full of grace and truth" (Jn 1:12-14).

17. St. Thomas treats predestination in his *Summa Theologiae* I pars, q. 23. See particularly article 5, ad 3. God allows some freely to damn themselves as a warning to the elect, who, if they were not warned, might also choose to damn themselves. In any case, his theological exposition respects the absolute sovereignty of God and his double attributes of justice and mercy. See also *CCC* 1037.

18. *CCC* 74, 843, 851, 1019, 1058.

19. "We know that by turning everything to their good, God cooperates with all those who love him, with all those he has called according to his purpose. They are the ones he chose especially long ago and intended to become true images of his Son so that his Son might be the eldest of many brothers. He called those he intended for this; those he called he justified, and with those he justified he shares his glory" (Rom 8:28-30).

4. RECONCILIATION LEADS TO HOLINESS

1. Pope John Paul II wrote in *Reconciliatio et Paenitentia,* n. 11: "The church has the mission of proclaiming this reconciliation and as it were of being its sacrament in the world. The church is the *sacrament,* that is to say, the sign and means of reconciliation in different ways, which differ in value but which all come together to obtain what the divine initiative of mercy desires to grant to humanity. She is a sacrament in the first place by her very existence as a reconciled community which witnesses to and represents in the world the work of Christ. She is also a sacrament through her service as the custodian and interpreter of sacred scripture, which is the good news of reconciliation inasmuch as it tells each succeeding generation about God's loving plan and shows to each generation the paths to universal reconciliation in Christ. Finally she is a sacrament by reason of the seven sacraments which, each in its own way, 'make the church.' For since they commemorate and renew Christ's paschal mystery, all the sacraments are a source of life for the church, and in the church's hands they are means of conversion to God and of reconciliation among people. Certainly a reading of scripture with regard to the passion of Jesus and his death on the cross reveals unmistakably how much God loves sinners" (Vatican City: Libreria Editrice Vaticana, 1984).

2. Note what was written early in chapter 1 about present perspectives: "Religion gets most of its strength from the fact that it enables individuals to feel good about themselves so that they can cope with the pressures that come from a highly competitive society."

3. "Son of man, I have appointed you as watchman for the house of Israel. When you hear a word from my mouth, warn them

for me. If I say to someone wicked, 'You will die,' and you do not warn this person; if you do not speak to warn someone wicked to renounce evil and so save his life, it is the wicked person who will die for the guilt, but I shall hold you responsible for that death. If, however, you do warn someone wicked who then fails to renounce wickedness and evil ways, the wicked person will die for the guilt, but you yourself will have saved your life" (Ez 3:17-20).

4. Myth, contrary to popular misconception, is not a kind of fairy story. In the scriptures, it is a literary form which is the expression of a truth that goes beyond what can be historically validated. For an extended explanation, see John L. McKenzie, S.J., "Aspects of Old Testament Thought," in *The Jerome Biblical Commentary* (Englewood Cliffs, NJ: Prentice-Hall, Inc., 1968), 77:23-24.

5. Gen 3:1-24; cf. chapter 1.

6. For a treatment of the subject of "original sin" with excellent references for further research, see Benedict M. Ashley, O.P., *Theologies of the Body: Humanist and Christian* (The Pope John Center, 1985), 385. Also cf. *CCC* 400, 402-409.

7. The apostle Paul tells us that everything in heaven and on earth was reconciled to one another and to God when Jesus made peace by his death on the cross (Col 1:20).

8. *Veritatis Splendor*, n. 70.

9. It should also be noted that the preacher and other members of the parish team have been equally shaped by American culture. It is not as if the preacher had an objectivity about sin that is above and beyond that of his or her listeners.

10. John Paul II, *Reconciliatio et Paenitentia*, n. 11.

11. Paul Johnson, *Modern Times: The World from the Twenties to the Eighties* (New York: Harper & Row, Publishers, 1983), 11.

12. John Paul II, however, gives a significant caution with regard to psychology: "While the behavioral sciences, like all experimental sciences, develop an empirical and statistical concept of 'normality,' faith teaches that this normality itself bears the traces of a fall from man's original situation—in other words, it is affected by sin....The behavioral sciences, despite the great value of the information which they provide, cannot be considered decisive indications of moral norms." *Veritatis Splendor*, n. 112.

13. *Op. cit.*, 139.

14. *Ibid.*, n. 21, 139.

15. Karl Menninger, M.D., *Whatever Became of Sin?* (New York: Hawthorn Books, Inc., 1973), 19.

16. See, for example, St. Thomas Aquinas, *Summa Theologiae*, I–II, q. 6, a. 4–8.

17. Not all biblical scholars are in agreement regarding the dating of Deuteronomy. It seems to have undergone a long period of formation, perhaps not ending until the middle of the sixth century B.C. Cf. Joseph Blenkinsopp, "Deuteronomy," in *The Jerome Biblical Commentary*, 6:4.

18. A nice appearance is one of the great attributes of the scam artist.

19. Hatred takes different forms. Today we describe the same reality as disdain for others, disrespect of persons, or self-centeredness. Not every act of hatred has to be premeditated murder to qualify as hatred. In all cases, the sinner elevates himself or herself above all others, including God. Those who hate act only for the benefit of themselves no matter what the consequences to others.

20. Until the death of the sinner, however, God wishes to lead that sinner back to himself. In fact, the whole purpose of Jesus' coming into the world was to call sinners to repentance. Cf. Mt 9:13; Lk 5:32; 15:7; Rom 5:8; 1 Tim 1:15.

21. Isaiah says of the Israelites of his day: "We know our iniquities: rebellion and denial of the Lord God, turning our back on him, talking treachery and revolt, murmuring lies in our heart" (Is 59:13).

22. *Dives in Misericordia,* n. 13 (November 30, 1980).

23. St. Thomas Aquinas discusses the hardening of the heart of the sinner in his description of how less serious (venial) sins dispose the sinner to sin more readily in serious (mortal) matters. This disposition occurs in two ways: (1) the lighter sins generate a habit of sinning which leads in time to more serious offenses; (2) the lighter sins remove inhibitions against sinning more seriously. With regard to the first, for example, the thief who gets into the habit of stealing small amounts of money successfully finds it much easier to steal larger amounts. The petty thief as a child can easily become a major felon as an adult. With regard to the second, for example, the one who gives in to his lust by self-abuse where no injustice is

done to another finds it easier to give in to his lusts for pornography where there are serious violations of justice. Cf. *Summa Theologiae*, I–II, q. 88, a. 3.

24. Cf. Gal 5:19–24 and Rom 6:13.

25. The First Letter of John applies this truth to the very specific circumstances of human relationships. It says: "Anyone who claims to be in the light but hates his brother is still in the dark. But anyone who loves his brother is living in the light and need not be afraid of stumbling, whereas the man who hates his brother and is in the darkness does not know where he is going, because the darkness blinds him" (1 Jn 2: 9–11).

26. Romans 7:14–24 is an excellent summary, almost clinical in its description, of the thought processes that go on in the mind of a person who sincerely resolves to do good but finds himself trapped in his own weakness.

27. See *CCC* 817, 953, 1869.

28. Two articles in particular are valuable in helping to come to an understanding of the trauma that divorce inflicts on the children: Joan R. DeMarchant, "Children of Divorce," in *New Catholic World* (Mahwah: Paulist Press, Sept/Oct, 1984), Vol. 227, No. 1361, 216–220; Barbara Mahany, "Daddy doesn't live here anymore," in *U.S. Catholic* (March 1986), 20–27.

29. One really must read the prophecy itself to appreciate the evil of the time: Amos 2:7, 8ff.

30. For Paul's understanding of this basic truth about God's love in dealing with human beings, see Romans 1:18–32.

31. See, for example, Matthew 3:12; 7:13–27; chapters 13 and 25.

32. The final judgment is not something God imposes on us like some tyrannical king. Judgment is simply the recognition of what we have become. Through a life of virtue on earth we have become holy—holy enough to enter into the presence of divine holiness for all eternity. On the other hand, a life of vice means that we have opted not to become holy and, therefore, Godlike. Because we refuse to become holy, we will not be able to rejoice in the presence of the eternal holiness. This is condemnation—we freely choose to live forever outside the divine holiness where eternal happiness is impossible, and we will know the folly of our choice.

33. *CCC* 1455.

34. It is common experience how difficult—in some cases impossible—it is to go on a diet, give up smoking, avoid sexual aberrations, or just have the will to organize one's day so as to get adequate exercise for basic health.

35. Ephesians 6:10-18 lists the weapons the Christian needs to use to overcome the power of sin.

36. Ephesians 5:1-6:9 is an excellent, although not exhaustive, summary of the self-discipline required to grow in holiness, which is the only way one can escape from the clutches of sin's power. See *CCC* 1734, 2015, 2340.

5. HOLINESS IS THE FOUNDATION OF THE MORAL LAW

1. The different kinds of law will be explained subsequently in the body of the text. Nevertheless the following brief schematization should facilitate the reader's ability to distinguish the different kinds of law under discussion (*CCC* 1952).

KINDS OF LAW
Eternal Law
(In God Himself)

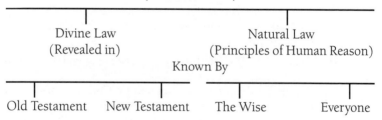

Divine Law	Natural Law
(Revealed in)	(Principles of Human Reason)

Known By

| Old Testament | New Testament | The Wise | Everyone |

2. *Summa Theologiae*, I-II, q. 93, a. 1; *CCC* 1951.

3. Cf. *ibid.*, I-II, q. 93, a. 3.

4. St. Thomas defines the natural law as those principles of human action found in the very nature of human reason which order these acts to their proper human end. Cf. *ibid.*, I-II, q. 90, a. 1, ad 2.; *CCC* 1954-1960.

5. Cf. Pope John Paul II, *Veritatis Splendor*, n. 50.

6. Cf. Gen 1:26-27.

7. *CCC* 1954-1955.

8. This word is used in scripture to describe those who are neither Jews nor Christians; it was used pejoratively. Today we prefer the term non-believers. With the Second Vatican Council, the Catholic Church reexamined its teachings regarding those religions not in the Christian tradition, stating in the *Declaration of the Church to Non-Christian Religions*: "The church is giving deeper study to its relationship with non-Christian religions" (n. 1) Then it made its affirmation of respect:

> Other religions to be found everywhere strive variously to answer the restless searching of the human heart by proposing "ways," which consist of teachings, rules of life and sacred ceremonies. The Catholic Church rejects nothing which is true and holy in these religions (n. 2). *The Documents of Vatican II*, ed. Walter M. Abbott, S.J. (New York: America Press, 1966).

9. Pope John Paul II, General Audience, September 9, 1998 in *L'Osservatore Romano* (Weekly Edition), No. 37, 16 September 1998, par. 2, p. 7.

10. St. Thomas Aquinas notes that not everyone is capable of understanding the natural law in all its aspects. Regarding some precepts of the natural law, only the wise (*sapientes*) are able to grasp them. This is the reason why the precepts of the natural law have been so controverted over the centuries. Cf. *Summa Theologiae*, I-II, q. 94, a. 2.

11. The parable about the Pharisee and the publican (or tax collector) is very much to the point here (Lk 18:10-14).

12. Cf. Col 2:20-23.

13. See also Mt 22:37-40.

14. *CCC* 2070-71.

15. God's will is his love for all his creatures, especially his chosen people.

16. *CCC* 1980.

17. Cf. Dt 31:16-18.

18. See also Lv 4:11-15.

19. *CCC* 1984.

20. Cf. *Summa Theologiae*, I-II, q. 91, a. 5 for St. Thomas' extensive and perceptive distinctions and relationships between the old and new laws.

21. I-II, q. 106, a. 1.

22. *Loc. cit.*, ad 1.

23. Sin is a word, deed or desire contrary to the eternal law *ST* I-II, q. 71, a. 6.

24. St. Thomas Aquinas treats of the nature and necessity of the divine law in his *Summa Theologiae*, I-II, q. 91, a. 4.

25. "The heart is more devious than any other thing, perverse too: who can pierce its secrets? I, Yahweh, search the heart, I probe the loins, to give each one what his conduct and his actions deserve" (Jer 17:9-10).

26. We refer the reader to the deleterious effects of psychiatry and psychology discussed previously in Chapter Four.

27. St. Thomas shows that conscience is an act of judgment by which a person decides whether or not what he is doing is in conformity with God's will. Cf. *Summa Theologiae*, I, q. 79, a. 13.

28. *CCC* 1781.

29. Cf. Rom 8:28-30.

30. Previously we discussed various kinds of guilt. Legitimate guilt occurs when the sinner recognizes the performance of a specific evil action which he or she did not have to perform. In other words, guilt occurs when the sinner recognizes that he or she has freely chosen a sinful thought, word, deed or action, the evil being specified by a real object that is contrary to the holiness of God. *ST* I, q. 71, a. 6.

6. HOLINESS MAKES FAMILY LIFE A REAL JOY

1. Pope Paul VI, Address to *Equipes de Notre Dame*, in *L'Osservatore Romano*, May 4, 1970.

2. *CCC* 303.

3. Psalm 119 illustrates this point well. It is a lengthy song of praise celebrating the glories of God's laws and describing the happiness they bring to those who obey them.

4. On the other hand, the prophets inveigh constantly against limiting cleanliness to ritualism. For them, worshiping with the lips while the heart is far from the meaning of the rite is religious hypocrisy. They insist that what is needed to be pleasing to God is a "clean heart" which is then reflected in ritual worship. Cf. Ez 36.

5. At the time of Jesus, the Jews were divided about resurrection. Since the Torah did not have any text explicitly affirming resurrection, the Sadducees denied it. They were of the priestly caste and religiously conservative. The Pharisees, on the other hand, accepted resurrection because they saw the law not as limited to the written Torah, but as developed by the oral Torah as well. This acceptance of oral tradition made them the liberals of their day. They were, therefore, in conflict with the Sadducees on the matter of resurrection. The dispute was particularly important in the persecution of Paul by the Jews, as described in Acts 23:1-10. Cf. Mk 12:18-27; Lk 20:27-40.

6. Any doubts raised in Jewish tradition regarding its inspired character were finally resolved by the Jewish council of rabbis at Jamnia in the first century A.D.

7. *CCC* 2332.

8. Cf. Paul VI, *Humanae Vitae*, July 25, 1968, n. 17.

9. *CCC* 1624, 2360.

10. The Book of Deuteronomy required that a man marry his brother's widow if she were childless in order to beget an heir to the brother's name and property. Cf. Dt 25:5-10.

11. The Catholic Church's extensive and detailed legislation about marriage contracts is an expanded articulation for the most part of the teaching of scripture. 1 Corinthians 7 and Ephesians 5:21-33 are particularly, although obviously not exclusively, significant.

12. *CCC* 2364, 2397.

13. The text is so important, I quote it here: "The Lord no longer regards the offering or accepts it with favor from your hand. "Yet you say, 'For what reason?' Because the Lord has been a witness between you and the wife of your youth, against whom you have dealt treacherously, though she is your companion and your wife by covenant. Let no one deal treacherously against the wife of your

youth. 'For I hate divorce,' says the Lord, the God of Israel" (Mal 2:14-16).

14. *CCC* 2365.

15. Later theological development identifies marriage as a sacrament: a symbol or sign of a hidden mystery in Christ which, at the same time, effects what it signifies. Thus, the sacrament of marriage gives the husband and wife the power to be faithful to their marriage vows even as Christ is faithful to his spouse the church.

16. "A man never hates his own body, but he feeds it and takes care of it in the same way that Christ treats the church, because we are its parts. For this reason a man shall leave his father and mother and be joined to his wife, and the two will become one flesh. This is a great mystery; but I am saying it applies to Christ and the church" (Eph 5:21-33).

17. Cf. *Gaudium et Spes*, n. 64.

18. While not an antidote to the pain, nevertheless faith knows that childless couples can still bear rich fruit for the Lord in charitable works, hospitality and sacrifice, and even adoption. Cf. *CCC* 1654, 2379.

19. *Gaudium et Spes*, n. 24, of the Second Vatican Council, compares selfless human love with the life of the Trinity: "There is a certain parallel between the union existing among the divine persons and the union of the sons of God in truth and love. It follows, then, that if man is the only creature on earth that God has wanted for its own sake, man can fully discover his true self only in a sincere giving of himself." *Vatican Council II: The Conciliar and Post Conciliar Documents*, Austin Flannery, O.P., ed., 1988 revised edition (Northport, NY: Costello Publishing Company), 925.

20. At the Last Supper Jesus said: "Unless I leave you [by my death on the cross], the Paraclete will not come to you; but if I do go, I will send him to you" (Jn 16:7). See also Jn 14:16: Jesus will ask the Father to send the Spirit when he goes back to the Father whence he came.

21. See especially Jn 3:13-17; 14:28-31; 17:1-5.

22. The Dominican theologian Benedict Ashley sums up the conclusions of many theologians on sexuality when he writes: "Sexual love is not understood as a means to procreation, nor is procreation seen merely as an incidental result of sex, to be avoided or promoted

according to individual subject preferences. Rather, procreation is seen as the expansion and completion of the couple's love for one another. Love, and only love, is the primary goal of sexuality, but sexual love by its specific nature is a fruitful love which demands its fulfillment not merely in orgasm, nor even in the exclusive relation of man and woman, but in the creative sharing of that love with new persons and the future. Normally this full meaning of sexual love is discovered experientially by the couple who find that their love for each other stirs profound longings to perpetuate this love beyond death in children in whom they will love again." Benedict M. Ashley, O.P., "A Theological Overview on Recent Research on Sex and Gender," in *Sex and Gender: A Theological and Scientific Inquiry*, eds. Mark F. Schwartz, et al. (St. Louis: The Pope John Center, 1984), 6.

23. *CCC* 2373.

24. "A study of couples practicing natural family planning conducted by family sociologist Virginia Heffernan in the Washington, D.C. metropolitan area in 1975 found that Catholics who were using the methods solely out of obedience to the church found it frustrating and destructive of their marriage relationship. On the other hand, deeply religious women, who chose natural methods both for religious reasons and because they are natural, expressed the greatest satisfaction of all women with the method." Mary Shivanandan, *Challenge to Love* (Bethesda: KM Associates, 1979), 100.

25. Paul in his First Letter to the Corinthians recognizes the power of the sexual drive: "On account of sexual immorality, every man should have his own wife, and every woman her own husband." The sense of Paul's teaching is that while everyone should remain as each is—so if single, remain single—excessive asceticism in marriage can lead to immoral behavior because of the intensity of the human sexual drive. He recognizes that both celibacy and marriage are gifts, and both should be respected (cf. 1 Cor 7:7). Nevertheless, if the unmarried cannot "control the sexual urges, they should get married, since it is better to be married than tortured" (1 Cor 7:9).

26. Natural family planning (NFP) as it is referred to here is not the "rhythm method" which was a rather primitive attempt to regulate births while remaining in harmony with nature. Today NFP

uses either the Billings Method or the Sympto-Thermal Method, or a combination of both. These methods are based on certain measurable (and variable) signs of a woman's fertility such as her basal body temperature and the consistency of mucous coming from the vagina. When properly applied after formal instruction by certified experts, the NFP is 98.8% effective—more effective, in fact, than the use of artificial means (*CCC* 2370).

27. Shivanandan, *op. cit.*, preface.

28. "Those marriages in which both spouses pray every day are almost twice as likely to be marriages in which both spouses say their sexual fulfillment is excellent." Steven Preister, "Marriage, Divorce and Remarriage in the United States," in *New Catholic World*, Vol. 229, No. 1369 (Jan/Feb 1986), 18.

29. *CCC* 2342-43.

30. *CCC* 2339.

31. Obviously, the same saying applies equally to women looking lustfully at men.

32. Compare the attitude reflected here to the beatitudes of Jesus in Matthew 5:1-12 and Luke 6:20-26.

33. So strong is the attraction of greed that Paul writes: "The love of money is the root of all evil, and there are some who, craving it, were led away from the faith, and so gave themselves many sorrows" (1 Tim 6:10).

34. Manicheism and other forms of dualism see the world divided into two principles of good and evil. Evil is that associated with the body; hence, to have intercourse is to do evil and propagate evil. This is not orthodox Christianity, however.

35. Cf. 1 Cor 7:1-40 where Paul considers a number of closely related questions on marriage and virginity.

36. Cf. *ST* II-II, q. 152, a. 2. For an excellent development of St. Thomas' teaching, see Servais Pinckaers, O.P., *The Sources of Christian Ethics*, trans by Sr. Mary Thomas Noble, O.P. (Washington: The Catholic University of America Press, 1995), 449-452.

37. John Paul II, *Pastores Dabo Vobis* March 25, 1992, n. 29. Vatican translation (Boston: St. Paul Books and Media), 56.

38. Cf. Rom 2:12-16.

7. HOLINESS RESULTS IN A HOLY LIFE-STYLE

1. Chapter 1, *passim.*

2. John Paul II, *Fides et Ratio* (*Origins*, Oct. 22, 1998, vol. 28, no. 19).

3. *Gaudium et Spes*, n. 7.

4. *Fides et Ratio*, n. 102

5. John Paul II, *The Vocation and the Mission of the Lay Faithful in the Church and in the World* (*Christifidelis Laici*), December 30, 1988.

6. *Veritatis Splendor*, August 6, 1993, n. 31.

7. George Gallup, Jr. and Jim Castelli, *The American Catholic People: Their Beliefs, Practices, and Values* (Garden City: Doubleday and Company, Inc., 1987), 4.

8. Thirty percent are in business or the professions (*ibid.*, 5) and 142 were members of Congress (*ibid.*, 4).

9. *Ibid.*, 5.

10. *Ibid.*, 3.

11. Unfortunately, and probably unjustly, contemporary social and economic conditions in many areas of the United States are forcing both spouses to get jobs to the detriment of family life, since one wage-earner simply cannot provide even the basics of a truly human family existence.

12. The rapidly increasing numbers of Hispanic and Asian Catholic refugees, of course, are not included at this time in the general overall prosperity of the earlier European immigrants. The former constitute 16% of the Catholic population, according to Gallup and Castelli (*op. cit.*, 3).

13. This is treated extensively in chapter 1.

14. *Ibid.*, 51.

15. The task, however, is made easier by what was reported in chapter 1. In spite of their own financial successes, Catholics as a whole are committed to social programs which help the less fortunate. This will be treated more fully in chapter 8.

16. It also means that the poor who are saved from pride by their poverty are blessed. It does not apply to those whose poverty leads them into sin.

17.   This is consistent with his subsequent teachings regarding the nature of being poor.

18.   Cf. Gen 1:28; Mt 19:3-11; 22:23-30.

19.   Gallup and Castelli, *op. cit.*, 6.

20.   *Ibid.*, 6.

21.   The comparable statistics for the years 1969 and 1998 are taken from *The Official Catholic Directory* (New York: P.J. Kenedy & Sons). In 1969 the total number of students under Catholic instruction was 10,969,483. No comparable figure is given for 1998.

22.   "On the basis of a fair number of interviews, I have the impression that most young priests do not want to work with young people. They argue that they are adult males, and they want to work with other adult males and not be tied down to the 'kiddie apostolate.'" Andrew M. Greeley, *New Horizons for the Priesthood* (New York: Sheed & Ward, 1970), 115.

23.   Cf. *Gaudium et Spes: The Church in the Modern World*, n. 50: "Marriage and married love are by nature ordered to the procreation and education of children. Indeed children are the supreme gift of marriage and greatly contribute to the good of the parents themselves." In *Vatican Council II: The Conciliar and Post Conciliar Documents*. Edited by Austin Flannery, O.P. (Northport, NY: Costello Publishing Company, 1975), 953.

24.   "Sons...are the first line of God-ordained human defence of the family in times of need....In more modern terms, one could venture to say that the alternative to a geriatric ward is a God-centered family." When sons are born in youth, "when the father gets old, his sons are about to reach their prime." From the commentary on the psalm by A. A. Anderson in *The Book of Psalms, Vol. 2, New Century Bible* (London: Oliphants, 1972), 868.

25.   The Second Vatican Council calls parents "the interpreter of God's love" (*Gaudium et Spes*, n. 50).

26.   John Paul II, *The Vocation and the Mission of the Lay Faithful in the Church and in the World (Christifidelis Laici)*, December 30, 1988, n. 34.

27.   Vatican Council II, *Decree on the Ministry and Life of Priests*, n. 6, in Walter M. Abbott, gen. ed., *The Documents of Vatican II* (New York: Guild Press, 1966).

8. HOLINESS LEADS TO SOCIAL JUSTICE

1. Because animals are not persons, in terms of the virtue of justice they do not have rights. This is also evident from the fact that animals kill and eat other animals. Predators are such by nature and are not deserving of punishment. Cruelty toward animals, therefore, is not a violation of their rights, but cruelty to any living thing, human or animal, is clearly a violation of human dignity which requires respect for all of God's creations. (See *Catechism of the Catholic Church*, No. 2418.) Even when animals are killed for food or used in medical research, they should be treated "humanely" (*CCC* No. 2417, 2457).

2. St. Thomas Aquinas, *Summa Theologiae*, II-II, q, 57, a. 1.

3. To treat the complex issues of social justice in specific detail is beyond the scope of this book. For a general overview and discussion of social justice issues and the teaching of the church, while not exhausting contemporary resources, the following are particularly helpful: *Catechism of the Catholic Church; Proclaiming Justice & Peace: Papal Documents from Rerum Novarum through Centesimus Annus,* ed. Michael Walsh and Brian Davies (Mystic, CT: Twenty-Third Publications, 1991); Pedro V. Salgado, O.P. *Social Encyclicals: Commentary and Critique* (Quezon City, PI: R.P. Garcia Publishing Co., Inc., 1992); Philip Land, "Justice: A Biblical Call," *The New Dictionary of Theology*, ed. Joseph A. Komonchak, et al. (Wilmington, DE: Michael Glazier, Inc., 1987), 549-553; Charles D. Skok, "Social Teaching of the Church," *The Modern Catholic Encyclopedia*, ed. Michael Glazier and Monika K. Hellwig (Collegeville: Liturgical Press, 1994), 814-815; Jose Maria Diez-Alegria, "Justice," *Encyclopedia of Theology*, ed. Karl Rahner (New York: Crossroad, 1982), 788-796; and Bishop Geoffrey Robinson, "Do We Know What Justice Is?" *Origins* 23 (1993), 423-430.

4. St. Thomas, *Summa Theologiae*, II-II, q. 58, a. 1.

5. *Ibid.*, II-II, q. 58, a. 11.

6. *Ibid.*, I-II, 49, 3.

7. "Each one has received a special gift, so, like good stewards responsible for all these different graces of God, put yourselves at the service of others" (1 Pet 4:10).

8. "It is all that is good, everything that is perfect, which is given us from above; it comes down from the Father of all light; with him there is no such thing as alteration, no shadow of a change" (Jas 1:17).

9. The Christian also owes duties of worship, praise and thanksgiving to God, but these duties transcend human justice. A person cannot pay to God all that is strictly due to God; there is no possibility of fairness or equality in the relationship. Nevertheless, by grace, the Christian has been given both the desire and the power to render to God something of what he is due; this rendering is called devotion, an act of religion. Cf. ST II-II, 80, 1; 81, 4; 82, 2.

10. St. Thomas treats these divisions in the whole of Question 58 of II-II in his *Summa Theologiae*.

11. For example, to act unjustly toward a person of a different race because of racial prejudice violates the rights of the individual, but it also has harmful ramifications for the whole race of which the person is a member. Racism, then, is made up of individual injustices, but it also results in consequences which harm society as a whole. The state, therefore, rightly legislates to prevent any form of individual injustice that would constitute racism. So today we see the state passing "hate" laws, anti-discrimination laws in housing and employment, and even laws requiring affirmative action as compensation for past injustices.

With regard to crime, "Prior to 1980, only five states had any type of statute related to bias crimes. Today, approximately thirty states have enacted measures dealing with bias crimes." For an excellent summary of the situation, see the article from which the above quote is taken: Charles Lewis Nier III, "241, Racial Hatred: A Comparative Analysis of the Hate Crime Laws of the United States and Germany," in *Dickenson Journal of International Law*, Winter 1995, especially footnote 171, citing statistics.

12. Michael Warner has written an interesting and provocative book on the bishops' efforts in the area of public policy which details the history of their approach. *Changing Witness: Catholic Bishops and Public Policy, 1917–1994* (Grand Rapids: William B. Eerdmans Publishing Company, 1995), (paper), p. 202.

13. The Ethics and Public Policy Center issued *Challenge and Response: Critiques of the Catholic Bishops' Draft Letter on the Economy,* 1995.

14. "If anyone loves me he will keep my word, and my Father will love him, and we shall come to him and make our home with him" (Jn 14:23).

15. For example, many of the injustices that are perpetrated in the world today stem not just from individuals but from the international economic structures. At the same time, since decisions establishing, modifying and changing structures are made, in the last analysis, by individual persons with power and influence, the responsibility for making the world more just is the work of individuals. Concerning the correction of these structures, Pope John Paul II has written: "The difficult road of the indispensable transformation of the structures of economic life is one on which it will not be easy to go forward without the intervention of a true conversion of mind, will and heart [of individual persons]. John Paul II, *Redemptor Hominis* (Redeemer of Mankind) (March 4, 1979) in *Proclaiming Justice & Peace: Papal Documents from Rerum Novarum Through Centesimus Annus,* ed. Michael Walsh and Brian Davies (Mystic, CT: Twenty-Third Publications, 1991), n. 18.

16. Pope John Paul II, *Dives in Misericordia (Rich in Mercy),* November 30, 1981 (Editrice Libreria Vaticana), n. 12.

17. *Ibid.,* n. 5.

18. "Mercy is manifested in its true and proper aspect when it restores to value, promotes and draws good from all the forms of evil existing in the world and in man." *Ibid.,* n. 6.

19. There have been a number of cases reported in the newspaper that illustrate this relationship between justice and love. Illegal immigrants have been given jobs and paid wages far below the legal minimum wage because the immigrants feared deportation and accepted whatever little money they could get without complaint. One woman gave an illegal immigrant a job as her maid at a very low wage. The maid took the job because she was desperate; she did not complain to anyone because she was afraid she would be deported. Now the employer claimed she was being charitable by giving the maid a job in the first place to help her out. But she was not charitable because she was unjust.

The hiring was unjust on two counts. First, it was against legal justice: hiring an illegal alien broke the law and, therefore, violated the state's right and duty to control immigration for the good of the resident population. Second, it was against commutative justice because the employee had no choice but to agree to the unjust wage; it was not a free contract. For these reasons, the employer was not charitable; on the contrary, she violated gospel love, because the terms of employment were unjust from the beginning.

The excuse the employer gave for paying such a low and illegal wage was that she needed to have domestic help she could afford in order to keep her own job. Her needs, as she perceives them, however, did not give her permission to violate the rights of another. Justice rests on rights, not on mere subjective needs. This case also illustrates that justice does not depend on how I feel about a particular law, but on the rights established by the law.

20. Vatican Council II, *Gaudium et Spes (Pastoral Constitution on the Church in the Modern World)*, n. 93.

21. See, for example, Mt 6:21; 12:34; 13:15; Lk 6:45; 10:27; 12:34, et al.

22. "You must therefore be perfect just as your heavenly Father is perfect" (Mt 5:48).

23. *Redemptor Hominis,* n. 9.

24. See the whole of Exodus 24 where God gives the foundational laws of their life as God's own people to the Israelites.

25. Cf. Mt 22:15-22; Mk 12:13-17; Lk 20:20-26.

26. Jn 19:10.

27. Benedict M. Ashley, O.P. gives a brief but excellent summary of contemporary legal theories regarding the foundations of justice and human (and animal) rights in *Living the Truth in Love: A Biblical Introduction to Moral Theology* (New York: Alba House, 1996), p. 277.

28. There is an irony here, since Paul and Peter were both martyred during the unjust persecution of Christians by Nero in 67 A.D.

29. Gen 3:1-24.

30. This is basically the same reason we are commanded to honor our father and our mother (Ex 20:12).

31. See *CCC* 309-314.

32. See *CCC* 390, 397, 398, 416–418.

33. It is vital for the contemporary Christian to realize that observance of the ten commandments without the fulfillment of their meaning by Jesus in Matthew 5:20-48 is insufficient for the salvation Jesus offers to those who believe in him.

34. Pope John Paul II, *Veritatis Splendor (Splendor of Truth)*. Editrice Libreria Vaticana, 1993, n. 12.

35. The Code itself is now accessible on the Internet at The United States House of Representatives, Internet Law Library. There are literally too many laws to count.

36. In a recent case, a woman owned an 18,300 square foot plot of undeveloped land in an area controlled by the Tahoe Regional Planning Agency. The agency prevented her from building a house on her property to protect Lake Tahoe without giving her any compensation for her land. After six years of litigation, involving both the Agency and the Clinton Administration, she was finally permitted by the Supreme Court of the United States to seek compensation for being barred from building on her own property. Source: The *Washington Times*, May 28, 1997, A4.

37. The trend began when Alan Bakke brought suit against the Regents of the University of California for discriminating against him in favor of less qualified non-white applicants solely because he was a white man when he sought admission to the medical school. The case eventually went to the Supreme Court (Regents of the Univ. of Cal. v. Bakke, 438 U.S. 265 [178]) which ruled in his favor, and he was admitted to the medical school from which he eventually graduated. Since that time, the decision has been cited in a number of cases to overturn affirmative action legislation. Cf. http://supct.law.cornell.edu /supct/cases/438265.htm, 10 Feb 1997.

On November 5, 1996, the voters of California adopted Proposition 209 which states: "The state shall not discriminate against, or grant preferential treatment to, any individual or group on the basis of race, sex, color, ethnicity, or national origin in the operation of public employment, public education, or public contracting." It was challenged by the American Civil Liberties Union but the challenge died when the Supreme Court denied their petition for certiorari. (http://www.cadap.org/synopsis.html)

38. Title 29, *United States Code,* Sections 201–219, especially Section 206.

39. In the gospel parable of the workers in the vineyard, it is important to note that the owner gave a just wage to all, and a generous bonus to some, a practice companies still follow today in rewarding especially hard workers.

40. This is where disputes arise among legislators in trying to arrive at a just legal standard: they are basically trying to reduce what is the fruit of a virtue to a law. Sometimes they are successful; sometimes they are not. Sometimes one group may think that they have arrived at the virtue, while another group does not. This is the essence of the debate over fairness.

41. *CCC* 2456.

42. Americans have been blessed with a stable form of government since the adoption of our Constitution; even the Civil War, for all its devastating loss of life and property, did not destroy American society. One might even go so far as to say that the war reaffirmed the American ideals, especially in regard to the equality of all people through the freeing of the slaves. Europe has not had the same experience of stability. The French Revolution and the unification of Italy in the nineteenth century and communism, fascism, Nazism, and the First and Second World Wars in the twentieth—all these were major disruptions of civil society and the social order. Since the papacy was also seriously affected by these disorders, it is not surprising that it reacted cautiously to the grave issues of justice raised by economic changes in society.

43. John Paul II, *Centesimus Annus (The One Hundredth Year)* (1987) in *Proclaiming Justice & Peace: Papal Documents from Rerum Novarum through Centesimus Annus,* ed. Michael Walsh and Brian Davies (Mystic, CT: Twenty-Third Publications, 1991), n. 5.4.

44. John XXIII, *Mater et Magistra (Mother and Teacher)* (1961) in *Proclaiming Justice & Peace: Papal Documents from Rerum Novarum through Centesimus Annus,* ed. Michael Walsh and Brian Davies (Mystic, CT: Twenty-Third Publications, 1991), n. 42.

45. Pope Paul VI, *Populorum Progresso (Progress of Peoples),* 1967, in *Proclaiming Justice & Peace: Papal Documents from Rerum Novarum through Centesimus Annus,* ed. Michael Walsh and Brian Davies (Mystic, CT: Twenty-Third Publications, 1991), n. 36. See

also two other important papal teachings on the family: Pope John Paul II, *Familiaris Consortio (On the Family)* (November 22, 1981); *Letter to Families* (February 2, 1994). In the latter the pope states: The family [is] that fundamental community in which the whole network of social relations is grounded from the closest and most immediate to the most distant....It is an institution fundamental to life of every society (n. 17).

46. See also Lev 19:9; 23:22; Dt 24:19; Ru 2.

47. Not only does Jesus feed the physically hungry, but this miracle is a foreshadowing of the Holy Eucharist by which Jesus feeds the spiritually hungry.

48. *CCC* 2439.

49. *CA* 52.

50. An early book on the subject is Susan M. Hartmann, *The Marshall Plan* (Columbus: C.E. Merrill Publishing Co, 1968). See also, John Gimbel, *The Origins of the Marshall Plan* (Stanford: Stanford University Press, 1976); Allen W. Dulles, *The Marshall Plan* (Providence: Berg, 1993).

51. *CCC* 1503, 1586, 1941, 2443, 2444, 2445. For further discussion of the principle "preferential option for the poor," see Warner, *op.cit.*, pp. 141-143.

52. John Paul II, *CA* 57.

53. *CCC* 2401, 2403.

54. "Nevertheless, in the objective order established by God, the right to property cannot stand in the way of the axiomatic principle that the goods which were created by God for all men should flow to all alike, according to the principles of justice and charity." *Mater et Magistra*, 43.

55. *CA* 48.

56. Cf. *Mater et Magistra* 55 and 63.

57. It should be stated at the outset that in the economic order first place must be given to the personal initiative of private citizens working either as individuals or in association with each other in various ways for the furtherance of common interests. *Mater et Magistra*, 51.

58. For example, see 42 USA PL 105-158, approved 2-13-98 by the US Congress: "§601. Purpose (a) In general: The purpose of this part is to increase the flexibility of states in operating a program

designed to— (1) provide assistance to needy families so that children may be cared for in their own homes or in the homes of relatives; (2) end the dependence of needy parents on government benefits by promoting job preparation, work, and marriage; (3) prevent and reduce the incidence of out-of-wedlock pregnancies and establish annual numerical goals for preventing and reducing the incidence of these pregnancies; and (4) encourage the formation and maintenance of two-parent families."

Individual states, like Colorado, have passed their own legislation to define eligibility standards, work requirements, benefit levels, and other elements that had been spelled out previously in federal law. See 27-JAN Coco. Law. 37; C.R.S.A.# 26-2-701.

59.   Poverty as a virtue was also considered in Chapter Seven.

60.   *CA* 57.

61.   *CA* 58.

62.   St Thomas, *Summa Theologiae*, II-II, q. 117, especially a. 4.

63.   The parish, of course, cannot lobby for a particular candidate; it is against both civil and canon law.

64.   See below.

65.   Although history is the story of peoples and nations, it is also the story of single individuals whose short span of life has made the story to be what it is. We have only to think of the influence of individuals like Alexander the Great, who died at 33, Nero, Charlemagne, Mozart, George Washington, Einstein, Stalin, Roosevelt, Jonas Salk, and Mother Teresa. The list goes on and on of individuals who have changed the world; they were not victims of historical forces; they literally made history instead.

66.   "Man's true identity is only fully revealed to him through faith, and it is precisely from faith that the church's social teaching begins. While drawing upon all the contributions made by the sciences and philosophy, her social teaching is aimed at helping man on the path of salvation....It proclaims God and his mystery of salvation in Christ to every human being and for that very reason reveals man to himself. In this light, and only in this light, does it concern itself with everything else: the human rights of the individual and in particular of the 'working class,' the family and education, the duties of the state, the ordering of national and international society, economic life, culture, war and peace, and respect for life from the

moment of conception until death." Pope John Paul II, *Centesimus Annus*, 1987, n. 54.

67. *Ibid.*, nn. 48, 49.

68. The story of Maximilian Kolbe's heroic resistance to Nazism and his ultimate death for the faith is a great witness in the contemporary world.

69. Pope Paul VI, *Apostolic Exhortation on Evangelization (Evangelii Nuntiandi)*, n. 18.

70. This principle is enshrined in the United States Constitution by the Tenth Amendment: "The powers not delegated to the United States by the Constitution nor prohibited by it to the States are reserved to the States respectively or to the people."

71. Pope John XXIII, *Mater et Magistra,* 1961, n. 53.

72. *Ibid.*, n. 44.

73. "In recent years the range of such intervention has vastly expanded to the point of creating a new type of state, the so-called welfare state. This has happened in some countries in order to respond better to many needs and demands, by remedying forms of poverty and deprivation unworthy of the human person. However, excesses and abuses, especially in recent years, have provoked very harsh criticisms of the welfare state, dubbed the 'social assistance state.' Malfunctions and defects in the social assistance state are the result of an inadequate understanding of the tasks proper to the state. Here again the principle of subsidiarity must be respected: A community of a higher order should not interfere in the internal life of a community of a lower order, depriving the latter of its functions, but rather should support it in case of need and help to coordinate its activity with the activities of the rest of society, always with a view to the common good." *CA* n. 48.3. *CCC* 1883.

74. *Justice in the World*, n. 49.

75. *Ibid.*

76. *Catholic Mind*, March 1972, Vol. LXX, No. 1261, p. 60

77. *Ibid.*, nn. 49-55.

EPILOGUE

1. Paul VI, *Evangelii Nuntiandi*, n. 14.
2. John Paul II, *Catechesi Tradendae*, n. 68.

3. John Paul II, *Catechesi Tradendae*, n. 67.

4. See Introduction.

5. To see what scripture says about the wisdom of our age, read Romans 1:18-32; 1 Corinthians 1:18-31; 2 Timothy 3:1-9; 4:3,4. We also considered some of the myths that permeate our culture today in Chapter One: excessive individualism and loss of a sense of community, a weakened sense of personal responsibility, especially in respect to the rights of others, confusion about truth, and morality.

6. Vatican Council II, *Sacrosanctum Concilium (Constitution on the Sacred Liturgy*, n. 11.

7. *Ibid.,* n. 13.

8. *CSL*, n. 61.

9. Letter to the Editors-in-Chief of the *New American Bible*, September 18, 1970.

10. *EN*, n. 46.

11. *Ibid.*, n. 41.

Bibliography

Ashley, Benedict M. *Living the Truth in Love: A Biblical Introduction to Moral Theology*. New York: Alba House, 1996.

————. *Theologies of the Body: Humanist and Christian*. St. Louis: The Pope John Center, 1985.

Robert N. Bellah, et al. *Habits of the Heart: Individualism and Commitment in American Life*. Berkeley: University of California Press, 1985.

Catechism of the Catholic Church. Vatican City: Libreria Editrice Vaticana, 1994.

Gallup, George, Jr. and Jim Castelli. *The American Catholic People: Their Beliefs, Practices and Values*. New York: Doubleday & Company, Inc., 1987.

Greeley, Andrew M. *New Horizons for the Priesthood*. New York: Sheed & Ward, 1970.

Johnson, Paul. *Modern Times: The World from the Twenties to the Eighties*. New York: Harper & Row, Publishers, 1983.

New Jerome Biblical Commentary. Eds. Raymond S. Brown *et al.* Garden City: Doubleday & Company, 1985.

Notre Dame Studies in American Catholicism. Notre Dame: Notre Dame University Press. (On-going)

The Official Catholic Directory. New York: P. J. Kenedy & Sons. (Yearly publication)

Origins (Washington, DC: NC Documentary News Service).

L'Osservatore Romano (Weekly Edition in English). Vatican City.

Pinckaers, Servais, O.P. *The Sources of Christian Ethics*. Translated by Sr. Mary Thomas Noble, O.P. Washington: The Catholic University of America Press, 1995.

Karl Rahner, ed. *Encyclopedia of Theology*. New York: Seabury Press, 1975.

Schillebeeckx, Edward. *Church: The Human Story of God*. New York: Crossroad, 1990.

Vatican Council II: The Conciliar and Post Conciliar Documents. Edited by Austin Flannery, O.P. Northport, NY: Costello Publishing Company, 1975.

Papal Documents

Collection:

Proclaiming Justice and Peace: Papal Documents from Rerum Novarum through Centesimus Annus, ed. Michael Walsh & Brian Davies. Mystic, CT: Twenty-Third Publications, 1991.

The following can be located as individual documents in a variety of editions by a variety of publishers:

Pope Paul VI. *Apostolic Exhortation on Evangelization in the Modern World (Evangelii Nuntiandi)*, 1976.

Pope John Paul II. *On Catechesis in Our Time (Catechesi Tradendae)*, 1979.

Dives in Misericordia (Rich in Mercy), 1981.

Familiaris Consortio (On the Family), 1981.

Reconciliatio et Paenitentia, 1984.

The Vocation and the Mission of the Lay Faithful in the Church and in the World (Christifidelis Laici), 1988.

Pastores Dabo Vobis, 1992.

Veritatis Splendor, 1993.

Letter to Families, February 2, 1994.

Fides et Ratio, October 22, 1998. In *Origins*, Vol. 28, No. 19.